# Engineer's Primer on Investing
### Financial Independence Retire Early (FIRE) v1.0

## Justin Masui

QUILL
HAWK
PUBLISHING

**Quill Hawk Publishing**

Published by Quill Hawk Publishing

ISBN: 978-1-965142-24-0 (Hardback)

ISBN: 978-1-965142-23-3 (Paperback)

Library of Congress Control Number: 2024921939

# Contents

"No man ever steps in the same river twice, for it's not the same river and he's not the same man." —Heraclitus

# Preface

Where to start? Where every journey starts: at the beginning! When posed with the question, "How much do I need to retire?" I was faced with the prospect of either 1) finding a financial advisor or 2) figuring out my retirement plans myself. As an engineer, I consider myself to be relatively numerate and, in a spate of typical engineering hubris (and no small amount of Dunning-Kruger[1]), I thought to myself: "How hard could this be?" After all, I had aced my accounting classes in college and had been investing since my teenage years. As I began my journey, it became clear that investing is a wide and deep field and has relationships with psychology, economics, politics, and probability. The deeper I went, the more I discovered other connections and a realization of my own psychological and intellectual limitations. To reflect the iterative and evolving nature of my financial journey, and in the proud tradition of software, I've annotated the subtitle with a version number.

This is not a "get rich" book, nor is it a guarantee of wealth – though my hope is that the reader will enjoy greater prosperity and a long life.[2] The same disclaimer applies from the start of this book to the end: the reader is ultimately responsible for their own financial choices and doing their own due diligence. To be clear, this book is not financial advice but a discussion of financial and investing concepts. The reader may apply similar concepts/ideas but is wholly responsible for their own outcomes. In other words, keep your lawsuits to yourself!

---

1. Kruger, Justin, and David Dunning. "Unskilled and Unaware of It: How Difficulties in Recognizing One's Own Incompetence Lead to Inflated Self-Assessments." Journal of Personality and Social Psychology 77.6 (1999): 1121.

2. Alpha, C. to M. (n.d.). Vulcan salute. Memory Alpha. https://memory-alpha.fandom.com/wiki/Vulcan_salute

# Introduction: How to Read This Book

This book was written with the mid-to-senior engineer in mind, so there are some technical and math terms that the reader is assumed to know as well as bits of science fiction topics/themes peppered throughout for good measure. However, that shouldn't preclude junior engineers or non-engineering folk from being able to get something out of this as long as there's a willingness to be open-minded and do a little bit of extra Googling.

Speaking of open-mindedness, this is probably the most essential requirement for reading this text. When I started my research, I quickly realized that one of my greatest strengths is my willingness to explore ideas that others might have veered away from due to political or moral affiliation. You don't have to do immoral things or take immoral stances – but you will need to accept that wisdom, regardless of its source, is worth giving some consideration. You don't have to like the people espousing a concept to understand the value of what they're saying.

What can be gained from this text is a summarization/overview of major investing concepts without having to read dozens of books/papers and relearning the same lessons that our smooth-brained ape brethren would otherwise pay dearly (probably in the form of thousands of dollars of lost principle) to learn from scratch. Similarly, if you came across a shipwreck, one of the first things you'd investigate is the black box or captain's log. How can you avoid a similar fate? What lessons/shortcuts can be gleaned from those who came before?

As such, this text is organized into four main sections:

1. Retirement Planning

2. Portfolio Construction

3. Essentials of Investing

4. Developing Alpha

Chapter 1 is all about personal finance – specifically, if one is trying to reach retirement, the steps that could be taken, such as budgeting and planning. If the reader has a firm grasp of these ideas they're welcome to skip this chapter in its entirety. It's included as a baseline for establishing common knowledge and goals.

Chapter 2 is about portfolio construction, i.e. beyond the basics of a 60/40 portfolio and examines alternatives and how to reduce risk through asset diversification. Again, if the reader has a firm grasp of these concepts then this chapter can be skipped as well. Caveat lector: I find that most folk don't have exposure to these ideas and often believe their portfolio to have much less risk than is reality.

Chapter 3 is where things get really interesting and the discussion turns towards different quantitative heuristics that can be applied to the investing domain.

Chapter 4 discusses the edge/alpha that can theoretically be achieved.

Chapter 5 is a bonus section where we give credit where it's due to the giants in the field and suggest additional avenues of investigation.

As personal finance can simultaneously be an emotionally challenging and relatively dry subject, it's reasonable to try to digest the contents of this text in small bites. Absorbing new concepts can take time. Internalizing and modifying one's perspective or view can take even longer. Cultivating patience and curiosity are key. As such, please recognize that the author is also on the same financial journey where he expects to encounter rough shoals and bitter weather in equal measure to fair weather and sunshine hope.

# Chapter 0: Attitudes About Money

Talking about money is a touchy subject for several reasons. Each and every one of us has some insecurities about money... and that's OK! We may have these insecurities because of the deep-seated ethos of the capitalist American Dream. Some folks misperceive money as society's valuation of an individual's worth – i.e., if I have more, I must be worth more, and conversely, if I have less money, I must be worth less. Some folk (too many) rightly see money in terms of survival (i.e., do I have enough to eat and live?). Others see net worth in terms of where that "ought" to be in the progression of their lives.

Those that come from a place of insecurity may take some solace that statistically the majority of us are probably more comparable in our lifestyles to each other than the uber wealthy or the 1%. Most folk figure wealth distribution to be quite uneven but are unaware of how vastly asymmetric that distribution really is in reality.

The following chart shows the distribution of wealth for Q4 of 2023 and 2011 based on data from FRED:[1]

---

1. Board of Governors of the Federal Reserve System (US), Share of Total Net Worth Held by the Bottom 50% (1st to 50th Wealth Percentiles) [WFRBSB50215], retrieved from FRED, Federal Reserve Bank of St. Louis; https://fred.stlouisfed.org/series/WFRBSB50215, April 20, 2024.

## Share of Total Net Worth Q4 2023 and Q4 2011

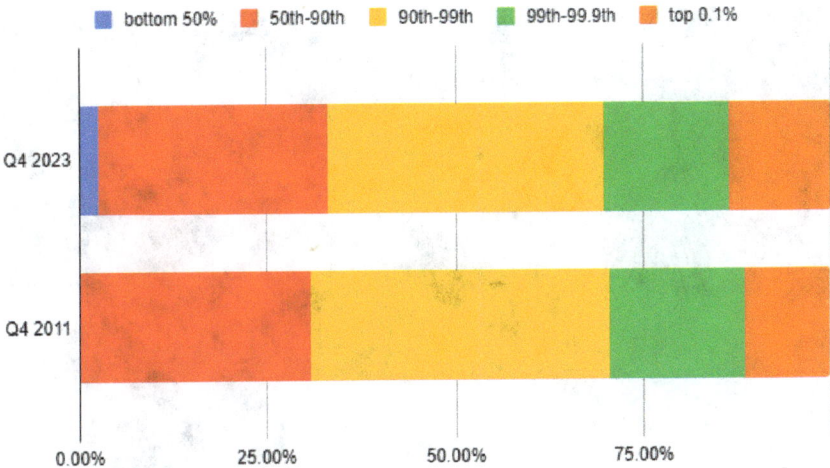

A couple of things to note:

- The bottom 50% owns just 2.5% of the wealth in 2023 and 0.04% in 2011.

- The top 10% owns about just a little under 70% of the wealth.

If you're comfortably in the middle class (i.e., around 50% of Americans), then your lifestyle is probably more similar to the bottom 15% than it is to the top 1%. This challenges the notion that anyone should look down their nose at someone for a relatively slight disparity in income or net worth. To be clear, this is not to say income equality isn't a critical issue or that fair pay isn't essential, but rather to point out that the vast majority of us are more alike than not. Hopefully, this will bring some comfort to those who are financially insecure that we're fighting right alongside you.

Moreover, discussing personal finances can be an anxiety-inducing discussion and the subject of significant relationship strain. Money represents – fairly or not – a significant projection of economic power. I've found that approaching challenging subjects through the lens of challenge-mastery[2] is key to overcoming the many would-be hurdles and a useful framework to detach emotionally from this subject.

2. Elliott, Elaine S., and Carol S. Dweck. "Goals: An Approach to Motivation and Achievement." Journal of Personality and Social Psychology 54.1 (1988): 5.

# Chapter 1: Retirement Planning

## 1.1 First Steps

There are many paths to financial independence and budgeting. What is presented here is merely one of many different approaches. What follows is a simple shortest-path conceptual approach. One doesn't have to follow these practices or adhere to the same process to get the same results. It's merely a model that, in the absence of extraneous circumstances/information, can help guide the retirement planning process.

When first considering a retirement plan, one might ask the following questions:

1. How much do I need to retire? (i.e., what is my number?)

2. How much do I spend on an annual basis? On a monthly basis?

3. How will my spending habits differ when I'm retired vs. now?

4. Do I need emergency money?

5. When can I retire?

6. Do I have significant sources of debt?

The quick answer to (1) is "as much as possible." It is generally ideal that one would want to retire with as much wealth as possible. But we can get more precision/accuracy if we reframe the question as what is the minimal amount of money I need to retire? This is "your number" – as it's referred to in the FIRE (financial independence retire early) community. To determine this number, we need to understand (2) how much do I spend on a regular basis?

There are a number of budgeting apps (discussed later) that can help answer this question.

Another key question to consider is: (3) Are my spending habits going to be the same as my spending habits later? Throughout this process, I'll need some emergency money (4) (i.e., a healthy buffer for unexpected expenses). Once 1–4 are known, we can finally begin to tackle (5) When can I retire? Given my current spending rate, I can estimate my savings rate. Lastly, (6) I'll need to account for any significant sources of debt. Maybe debt should be handled first, but I can simply add the amount of debt to my total "number" to get how much I need to save in order to retire.

The below dependency diagram summarizes the above questions:

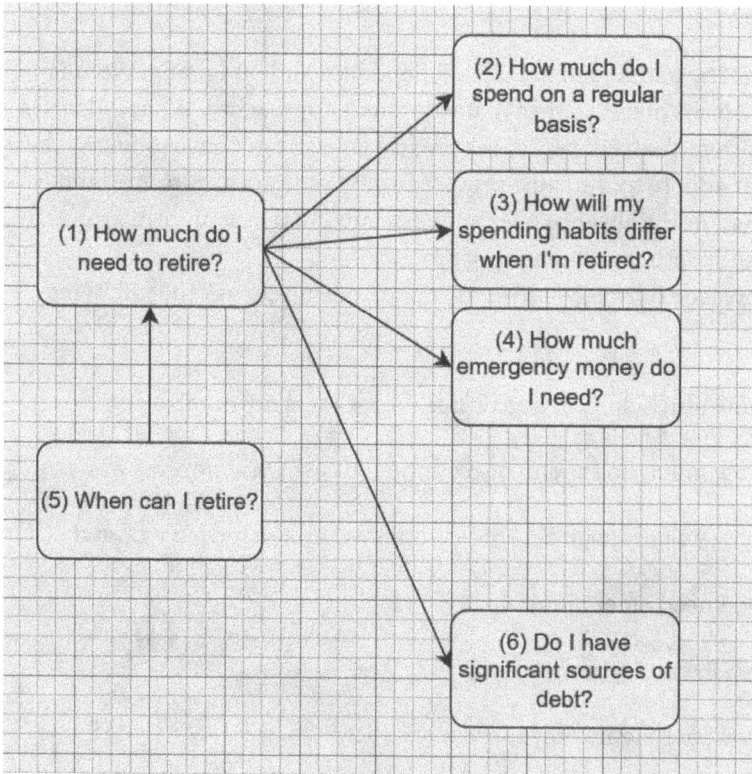

As Stephen Covey says, put "first things first."[1] So, we start by understanding our current spending rate.

---

1. Covey, Stephen R. *The 7 Habits of Highly Effective People*. Simon & Schuster, 2020

## 1.1.1 Tracking Expenses (Question 2)

In the long before time, when dinosaurs still ruled the earth, men (and women) etched their crude numeric pictographs with hardened carbon onto sheets of compressed plant matter to record their transactions in a painstaking and often error-prone process called "writing." Now, we have apps that do this automatically.

**Spreadsheets** – require far more discipline to track items on a monthly basis as each individual expense must be recorded manually. This manual process is prone to errors, whereas expense-tracking applications automatically import data from data sources such as banks.

**Rocket Money**[2] – Rocket Money has a free tier and a premium tier. Both of these apps are great for retroactively viewing how expenses are related to how much of a particular budget has been expended vs. preallocating as in the case of YNAB.

**YNAB**[3] – (which stands for "you need a budget") is a budgeting tool with an annual subscription fee. The benefit of YNAB over the aforementioned tools is that it allows for forward planning (i.e., every dollar is assigned a job). It also has higher real-time flexibility in that if you exceed a certain budget, you compensate by drawing money from another line item. As a user, you are required to be conscious of the tradeoff of going over budget. There is a bevy of tutorials that teach how to use the YNAB way of thinking about budgeting. An additional benefit of YNAB is that it uses double-entry accounting – a technique invented in Roman times to keep track of transactions. This helps reduce errors in accounting and shows the flow of money from one line item to another.

Whatever mechanism is used to track expenses, it's important to have a large enough sample size of data to have a realistic idea of typical expense behavior. A year is about sufficient time to gather a full picture of annual expenses across different times and holidays (i.e., to account for seasonality in expense behavior). To be clear, a full year of data isn't needed to get started on budgeting/planning. Starting from a week or month is sufficient to project expense behavior forward in time. The advantage of a larger amount of data

---

2. https://www.rocketmoney.com/

3. https://www.ynab.com/

is that it will give a more accurate long-term picture of expense behavior. The more data, the better because we'll discover expenses that we hadn't planned on, e.g., a gift for a friend graduating, that last-minute concert at the Gorge, or that tactical backpack that's really overpriced but you just need.

The Hershfield and Bartels study, "The Future Self,"[4] outlines how people tend to treat their future selves as a distinct persona. For this reason, initial forward-looking budgets will almost certainly be incorrect. Therefore, proper budgeting requires flexibility to accommodate unexpected life changes and expenses. Apps like YNAB and Mint accommodate this flexibility by allowing users to easily create additional expense categories. Additionally, it's helpful to create separate line items as buffers in the event of expense overruns.

Being new to budgeting or never having had a budget can be an exercise in fiscal self-discipline. Having discipline means staying within the budget, but it can't be so rigid that it's incapable of change. Life is full of change, so a budgetary mechanism needs to be similarly flexible regardless of whether it's an app or spreadsheet. Whatever mechanism is used, it needs to be intended for long-term use. Ease of use, low overhead, and exportable history are desirable traits. Further, the budget mechanism should be durable, i.e., if a computer or hard drive dies, there ought to be a backup. Cloud backups are especially attractive for this reason – though, of course, they come with a tradeoff between privacy and security.

### 1.1.2 How Will My Spending Habits Change When I Retire? (Question 3)

As the Smokey Bear adage goes: "Only you can decide your spending habits." Let's assume that you've identified that your current spending habits are fairly comparable to your retirement spending. If you intend to spend prodigiously, then that changes the calculation. Most studies (discussed later) assume a fairly comparable spend rate, or maybe less, depending on whether their simulation includes housing expenses or not.

---

4. Hershfield, Hal E., and Daniel M. Bartels. *"The Future Self."* The Psychology of Thinking About the Future. The Guilford Press, 2018: 89–109.

### 1.1.3 How Much of an Emergency Fund Do I Need (Question 4)?

Advice for this seems to change with the current unemployment rate. Typically, the rule of thumb for the amount of emergency living expenses is three months of cash on hand (i.e. in an easily accessible and secure location). In times of high uncertainty, the recommended number is usually six months of living expenses. Of course, in a high-credit society, such as the U.S. or South Korea, the average personal savings rate is at an all-time low. This is probably the result of the aforementioned phenomenon of people disconnecting their present selves from their future selves. Note: these questions are not necessarily in order of savings priority. Generally, most personal finance "experts" advocate paying down debt rather than paying into an emergency fund. We'll leave this prioritization as an exercise for the reader, as there's already a cornucopia of advice on this topic.

### 1.1.4 Calculating My Retirement Number (Question 1)

Let's say we've calculated our average annual expense and accounted for paying off debt and an emergency fund. We still need to determine how long our "number" will last while in retirement while taking into account inflation, taxes, and capital gains (presumably from investments).

There are several studies in this area, with folk doing various simulations and studies. Probably the most famous is the William P. Bengen (incidentally, an aeronautical engineer graduate from MIT) 1994 paper[5] that posits a safe annual withdrawal rate of 4% in retirement with a 50/50 stock/bond split. The heuristic for the 4% withdrawal rate is the "25x rule," or 25 times our annual expense rate. If we expect to spend $75,000/yr in retirement, then we'd need $75,000 * 25 = $1.875m. The "25x rule" is derived from the 4% withdrawal rate because 4% of something multiplied by 25 gets us back to 100% of the original amount. From our prior example, 4% of $1.875m is $75,000.

The Bengen study has the following features:

---

5. Bengen, William P. "Determining withdrawal rates using historical data." *Journal of Financial Planning 7.4 (1994): 171–180.*

1. It uses historical data between 1926 and 1976 with three major stock drawdowns.

2. It simulates the impact of different withdrawal rates between 3% and 6%.

3. It simulates the impact of different distributions of stock/bond splits, e.g., 50/50, 60/40, etc.

4. It accounts for the real rate of return (i.e., compensated for inflation).

If we examine Bengen's paper critically:

1. It has a stock market/bond dataset from about 1929 onward (i.e., a period over which the U.S. has had a long run of relative economic prosperity and growth).

2. There is a consistency of client behavior on a relatively constant withdrawal rate (i.e. it is assumed the client is disciplined enough to keep a constant withdrawal rate). He notes these behaviors in his discussion of "Black Holes" and "Stars" as extremes of client outcomes that result in significant loss and gain respectively.

3. Funds are assumed to be held in tax-deferred accounts.

The "Trinity Study"[6] [7] further reinforced the 4% rule when examining portfolio failure rates. They found that the withdrawal rate of 3–4% had a low probability of failure, might be too conservative and could cause investors to unnecessarily lower their standard of living. Below are tables based on data from the aforementioned Trinity study outlining the success probability at different withdrawal rates adjusted for inflation after 20 years and 30 years respectively.

---

6. Cooley, Philip L., Carl M. Hubbard, and Daniel T. Walz. "Retirement Savings: Choosing a Withdrawal Rate That Is Sustainable." *AAII Journal* 20.2 (1998): 16–21.

7. Cooley, Philip L., Carl M. Hubbard, and Daniel T. Walz. "Sustainable Withdrawal Rates From Your Retirement Portfolio." *Financial Counseling and Planning* 10.1 (1999): 39–47.

| Portfolio Success Rates from 1926 to 1995 after 20 Years | | | |
|---|---|---|---|
| | Withdrawal Rate | | |
| Portfolio Composition | 4% | 6% | 10% |
| 100% stocks | 100% | 75% | 33% |
| 75% stocks, 25% bonds | 100% | 75% | 27% |
| 50% stocks, 50% bonds | 100% | 75% | 10% |
| 25% stocks, 75% bonds | 100% | 47% | 4% |
| 100% bonds | 90% | 20% | 2% |

| Portfolio Success Rates from 1926 to 1995 after 30 Years | | | |
|---|---|---|---|
| | Withdrawal Rate | | |
| Portfolio Composition | 4% | 6% | 10% |
| 100% stocks | 95% | 68% | 34% |
| 75% stocks, 25% bonds | 98% | 68% | 7% |
| 50% stocks, 50% bonds | 95% | 51% | 0% |
| 25% stocks, 75% bonds | 71% | 20% | 0% |
| 100% bonds | 20% | 12% | 0% |

Based on these tables one might arrive at the conclusion that 4% is a relatively safe withdrawal rate. However, both of these papers depend on historical data to make their cases for forecasts – meaning that outcomes depend heavily on stock market behavior and the major assumption that past performance is a reasonable proxy of future behavior.

Even if a 3–4% withdrawal rate may be too conservative, from a planning perspective to improve the chances of an unpredicted economic disaster or other unplanned major expenditure it is reasonable to use a conservative number. For this reason, and despite critiques, the 25x rule remains a popular heuristic in the personal finance/retirement planning world in calculating one's "number."

### 1.1.5 Debt and Net Worth (Question 6)

Individuals aren't businesses, but sometimes it helps to conceptually view personal finances as a balance sheet analogue.

- Businesses: Assets – Liabilities = Equity

- Personal Finance: Assets – Debt = Net worth

Assets include fungible things like bonds, stocks, real estate, cars, etc. Liabilities include things like mortgages, student debt, and credit card debt. High debt/liabilities have a significant impact on net worth. Typically, intangible assets such as education aren't considered assets in this calculation, even if they're debt-financed and a good life choice, because they are not immediately and easily exchanged for money.

On the other hand, buying a house could be considered a debt-financed asset acquisition because a house could be sold in a relatively short time. The net worth of a real estate asset is determined by taking the value of the house for which it could currently be sold on the open market and subtracting the remaining left on the mortgage. Depending on purchase goals and how/why real estate was purchased, it may or may not be included as part of net worth. For instance, one might consider a primary residence as separate from net worth if it has extreme sentimental value and there is no intention to sell under any circumstances (e.g., a family property owned for generations). Alternatively, one might consider real estate as an investment, and therefore, it might make sense to consider it an asset because of an intent to sell.

## 1.2 Types of Accounts

### Pre-tax vs Post-tax

At this point, the differences between 401k, Roth, Roth 401k, traditional IRA accounts, and the associated variants (e.g., 457 and 403b, and Thrift and Savings Plans) should be pretty familiar to the reader. If they're not, it's worth a quick Google before proceeding. The purpose of these types of accounts is to shelter assets from taxes. The benefit of a post-tax account (e.g., a Roth IRA) is that it allows one to accumulate significant assets and not pay taxes on withdrawals at retirement. If a set of investments is expected to have a significant upside, then a Roth IRA makes the most sense. On the other hand, contributions made to a pre-tax account (e.g., 401k or traditional IRA) that would otherwise be in a higher tax bracket may be withdrawn at a lower tax rate, thereby increasing the tax savings.

*Example*: Say we have $20k that would've been taxed in the 30% tax bracket, but instead we contributed that $20k pre-tax account, it made no gains, but we withdraw when we retire at a 10% tax bracket: we pay $2k vs. $6k. Similarly, if we took that $20k now as post-tax at the 30% tax rate, we'd be left with $14k to invest. The advantage of pre-tax is predicated on the fact that the real value of money now is worth more than later due to inflation, and our withdrawal tax rate is lower than our contribution tax rate.

A caveat of pre-tax accounts is an RMD (Required Minimum Distribution). This is the minimum amount required to withdraw from a traditional IRA at a certain age.

*Example*: At present, if we're 72 and our IRA has $100k, and the distribution period is 27.4,[8] we'd need to withdraw 100k/27.4 = $3649.

The distribution period changes every year, and, additionally, depending on Congress, it will change over time. Roth IRA doesn't have an RMD (as of 2024 – make sure to check the rules as these are subject to frequent change).

The tax benefits from pre-tax are significant in two ways:

1. Rebalancing a portfolio doesn't incur a tax penalty on any capital gains.

2. During withdrawal (assuming a lower tax bracket), taxes on withdrawals will be lower.

### Passing on an IRA or Roth IRA as Inheritance

This might be worth considering if there are progeny involved (i.e., how will offspring handle an IRA inheritance or a Roth IRA). If it's a Roth IRA, kids or a spouse are in the clear, i.e., no taxes need to be taken out. A traditional IRA, on the other hand, is subject to taxes on distributions. The rules on this are complex, so it's worth seeking out a financial advisor to decide the optimal tax situation. The worst thing to do is to take out a lump sum and take a healthy haircut from the IRS – though given the presently historically low-income tax brackets of the top 1%, this might be a desirable choice.

---

8. https://www.irs.gov/retirement-plans/plan-participant-employee/retirement-topics-required-minimum-distributions-rmds

## Health Savings Account (HSA)

HSA, or Health Savings Account, is a type of account that allows one to save for health expenses. Himmelstein[9] found that 62% of 2007 bankruptcies in the U.S. were medical. Kelley[10] found that for 25% of senior citizens in the last five years of life, out-of-pocket expenses exceeded household assets. Additionally, the cost of healthcare rises significantly year over year. It's no wonder that investment in health-related equities has done so well in recent years.

HSAs have a triple benefit in taxes:

1. contributions reduce taxable income

2. contributions are made pre-tax

3. earnings aren't taxed on withdrawals for qualified medical expenses.

The contribution limits seem to change frequently, so it's a necessity to consult the IRS for the latest information. As of 2022, the contribution limit was $3650 and slated to rise to $3850. Most HSAs will have some set of limited investment funds they can invest in; in my case, they're broad-based index funds.

If the intention is to have some portion of the portfolio allocated to index funds, then an HSA may be a good alternative tax-advantaged account. If one is over 65, one can withdraw from an HSA without penalty (although the withdrawal is taxable as regular income). This is incidentally a reason to consider an HSA as part of one's net worth. On the other hand, including an HSA as part of a retirement nest egg may disincentivize one psychologically from necessary proactive health spending, e.g., buying that thermometer that really ought to be replaced. In my opinion, health is about taking proactive measures, so it makes sense to track health expenses and assets separately.

Another consideration and benefit of the HSA is that medical expenses can be reimbursed from the HSA account as long as the expenses incurred were

9. Himmelstein, David U., et al. "Medical bankruptcy in the United States, 2007: results of a national study." American journal of medicine 122.8 (2009): 741–746.

10. Kelley, Amy S et al. "Out-of-pocket spending in the last five years of life." Journal of general internal medicine 28.2 (2013): 304–309. doi:10.1007/s11606-012-2199-x

after the establishment date of the account. One can let the HSA account accumulate in value over the years and then take a reimbursement in the future.

*Example*: Suppose your HSA has $6000 in it, and you have a qualified medical expense of $2000. Let's take two scenarios:

1. *Pay the $2000 out of your HSA, so that leaves $4000 in the HSA:* Let's say after a few years it doubles in value. So, then there's $8000 in the HSA.

2. *Pay the $2000 out of pocket, thereby leaving $6000 in the HSA*: Same as scenario A, after a few years, the investment doubles so there's $12,000 in the HSA. After a reimbursement, $10,000 is left in the HSA.

Presuming a positive return on investment means more tax-free dollars in the HSA as in scenario B. It's key to keep receipts for those out-of-pocket expenses as required by the IRS. This incentivizes paying out of pocket for medical expenses in order to grow one's HSA account.

If one uses HSA funds for any other reason than eligible health expenses, it will be taxed as ordinary income and come with a 20% penalty. As stated above, medical expenses later in life are almost a foregone conclusion, so it makes sense to include them as part of long-term retirement plans. Additionally, an HSA can be passed down to descendants. Contributing to an HSA is an all-round winning choice!

Some HSA plans have administrative fees for investment choices. There may be some benefit from transferring a company-administered HSA to another low-fee HSA bank (e.g. Fidelity). In such a case, it is possible that the assets may need to be liquidated prior to that transfer.

### 529's

A 529 Plan is a type of account for educational expenses for a designated beneficiary. It's similar to a Roth IRA in that contributions are made after tax and can grow tax-free. However, the major difference is that withdrawals must be used for college expenses such as tuition, room & board, books, and supplies. Withdrawing from a 529 for non-college-related expenses will incur taxes on earnings as well as a 10% penalty, so there's a strong incentive to use funds for college-related expenses. It's possible to designate oneself as a beneficiary and withdraw for later education, as it can be used for graduate schools as well as professional schools. Check https://ope.ed.gov/dapip/#/home to see if a target school applies. 529s make sense as a tax shelter only if it's likely the funds will be used for college-related expenses.

Some 529 funds charge fees. For example, at the time of this writing, Charles Schwab charges a 0.2–0.86% annual fee, depending on the investment selected.

States may offer their own 529 program with different benefits from commercial institutions. For example, in WA, one can open a GET 529 account and buy GET units, whose future value of a college credit is guaranteed by the state. These credits can be used at other schools in the U.S., but if the cost of the college credit exceeds the cost of the University of Washington or Washington State University, then you must pay the difference. If it is less, then the remaining GET value can be used for other college-related expenses. If the GET units are not used, they can be transferred to another family member, or a refund may be requested. Refunds have the same penalties as withdrawing from a regular 529. WA also offers a DreamAhead 529, which seems to be the same as a commercial 529 but with less investment options than say a Charles Schwab 529.

The downside of investing in a 529 is that there is a risk that state governments change policies and laws. Additionally, a state government's fiscal situation can also change. Over a long-time horizon (e.g., 18 years), this level of trivial short-term risk may be undesirable (529s were introduced in 2013, so they are only ten years old!). There's also the opportunity cost of investment in GET, i.e., a 30% increase in the last 10 years seems like a lot, but consider the current annual rate, which is about 2–3% per year when compared to the annual return of investment in the S&P of 6–8% per year. Inflation, on average, is 3.8% per year. So, it is possible to get a risk-free real rate of return of -0.08% per year, compared to a slightly higher 2–4% real rate of return in an index S&P fund.

On the other hand, if the cost of education is examined from a longer time frame, there is a dramatic increase in cost of about 1200% since the 1980's. The below chart from the BLS displays an index of College tuition and fees.

**Consumer Price Index for All Urban Consumers (CPI-U)**

**Series Id:**     CUUR0000SEEB01
Not Seasonally Adjusted
**Series Title:**   College tuition and fees in U.S. city average, all urban consumers, not seasonally adjusted
**Area:**          U.S. city average
**Item:**          College tuition and fees
**Base Period:**   1982-84=100

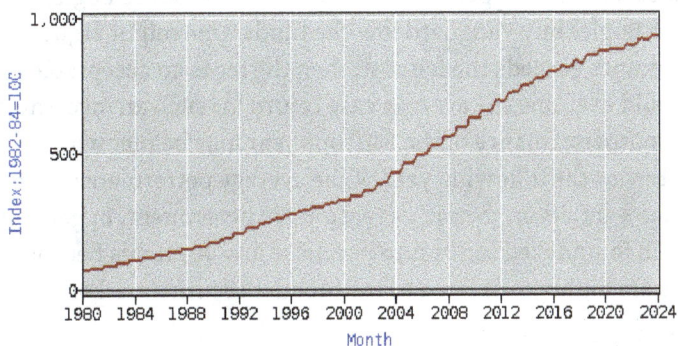

Source: https://data.bls.gov/timeseries/CUUR0000SEEB01?output_view=data

The reasons for this increase in cost, as explained in Visual Capitalist,[11] are:

- decrease in state funding

- increase in demand

- increase in Federal aid

In this context, a long-term investment in college funding may make sense.

### Bane of Fees
Different accounts may have small fees associated with them. These seemingly small fees can add up to quite a bit over time if not managed properly. These are often in the form of "administration fees" or "record-keeping" fees. There's no benefit from these fees, and they are a cost

---

11. Bhutada, Govind. "The Rising Cost of College in the U.S." Visual Capitalist, 4 Feb. 2021, www.visualcapitalist.com/rising-cost-of-college-in-u-s

against the investor's bottom line. Significantly, a vast majority of indexes, ETFs, and mutual funds have fees associated with them. These are usually a percentage of the principal investment taken off the top regardless of fund performance. If the S&P performs on average 6–8% per year and inflation is about 3–4%, then the real return is 3–4% per year. A fee of a few percent can be a significant part of real gains in a given year, e.g., a 1% fee can be as much as 25–33% of real gains. This is one reason that the Bogleheads (fans of John Bogle) buy Vanguard low-fee funds. One might argue that if a fund performance exceeds the fee cost, then the fee is an acceptable price to pay. We should examine the average case return for such an investment and whether its outperformance of the S&P one year may be met with reversion to mean behavior the following year. If the average performance far exceeds the cost in fee + inflation, then it's a reasonable investment. In general, the rule of thumb for indexed funds is to purchase low-fee funds because the alternatives are highly correlated to the broader security market.

## 1.3 Retirement Contributions

### Saving Tips

The concept of "hedonic adaptation" is that we get a little bit of a dopamine boost initially from an increase in quality of life, but our brains correspondingly grow accustomed to that increased quality of life such that we no longer get the same boost. We need to spend more hard-earned dollars to get the corresponding dopamine injection. The practical implication of personal finance is that folk tend to spend up to the limit of their income. Developing a scarcity mindset can help prevent ballooning expenses over time associated with increases in income. Another method of mitigating the threat to savings from the hedonic treadmill is to automate that saving by automatically transferring the intended savings amount to the intended account. This has two main benefits:

1. It is psychologically less effort because it doesn't feel like giving up something.

2. It takes less time because the transfer is automatic vs manual.

Automation from one account to another, or an automatic contribution to a 401k or other retirement account type, is ideal for this benefit. Automatically contributing to a retirement account has the added benefit of being more difficult to withdraw without penalties, so those savings are less likely to be spent on spontaneous whims.

### Dollar Cost Averaging

If a large single lump sum investment seems intimidating, another approach is to use Dollar Cost Averaging (DCA), which is a fancy way of investing in a desired asset at fixed amounts periodically over time.

*Example*: If a $100,000 allocation into a U.S. Index Fund is needed, then auto invest every week for $2000 and fully deploy the principle in a little less than a year.

Aside from the psychological benefit of not putting all one's eggs in a single basket, it takes out the temptation of timing purchases to the short-term price action of the asset, i.e. not purchasing because the price seems to be moving upwards/downwards and possibly missing out on a longer-term positive trend (e.g. S&P has a positive bias).

### Backdoor Roth Contributions

A Backdoor Roth contribution is a method to contribute to a Roth if one's income exceeds the Roth IRA income contribution limit. Contributions to Roth IRA contributions are capped based on an income limit, which seemingly changes every year (single: $153k/year or joint: $228k/yr. as of 2023).

The idea is to contribute to a traditional IRA the maximum allowable annual amount ($6k as of 2023) after-tax dollars and then convert that contribution to Roth. The catch is that if the $6k is claimed as a deductible to traditional and subsequently converted to Roth, then taxes need to be paid on the contribution. On the other hand, if the contribution to the traditional IRA is made with after-tax money, then that amount can be converted to a Roth without a tax penalty, but the contribution cannot be claimed as a deductible. This allows high-income earners to accumulate wealth in their Roth IRA.

Note: One shouldn't blindly convert pre-tax traditional IRA dollars to Roth IRA because of the potential of paying taxes on the conversion amount.

### Mega Backdoor Roth Contributions

A Mega Backdoor Roth Contribution isn't available to everyone, so consulting a retirement plan administrator will confirm whether this is a valid option. The basic idea is that $43,500 (as of 2023) can be contributed to an "after-tax" account (separate from a 401k pre-tax account). As soon as funds are in the after-tax account, then one can request an "in-plan" conversion from the "after-tax" account into a Roth IRA. Depending on a company's retirement plan administration, there should be a way to see the breakdown of pre-tax and post-tax accounts. If an in-plan conversion is done immediately after a contribution, it's likely no taxes will have to be paid on any earnings. On the other hand, if "after-tax" contributions have earnings, then taxes will have to be paid on the conversion amount. Some administrators will do this conversion automatically. Depending on investment performance, this mechanism could save tens of thousands in taxes over the lifespan of the account.

### Order of Operation in Account Contributions

While everyone's financial situation is a little bit different by virtue of lifestyle and cost of living, there are some broad guidelines that can be followed to optimize retirement outcomes:

1. contribute to pre-tax accounts first (i.e., the 401k, traditional IRA, HSA, etc.) in order to reduce taxable income as much as possible

2. contribute to post-tax accounts, e.g. Roth IRA and 401k Roth

This ordering is generally desirable under the assumption that the tax savings on contribution is greater than the tax rate on withdrawal. In such a case, the excess savings has an investment accumulation that can have slightly better outcomes when factoring in inflation and taxes. On the other hand, if the expectation is to be in a higher tax bracket, then it makes sense to use a Roth IRA where withdrawals are tax-free.

Typically, a retiree is withdrawing at a lower tax rate – ideally when they have no other income and are below the standard deduction.[12]

Below is a simple simulation of the performance of a *single $19,500 contribution* under different macroeconomic conditions contrasting pre- and post-tax accounts. These scenarios range from very pessimistic where capital growth is negative and inflation is high to optimistic where we have good capital growth and low inflation.

First, we start with our assumptions for different scenarios:

---

12. https://www.madfientist.com/traditional-ira-vs-roth-ira/

- Assume an income tax bracket of 22% because it's about in the middle of the tax brackets to compare between a high-income tax bracket and a low-income tax bracket

- Annual Gain (Appreciation) at different levels

- Annual Inflation at different levels

- Calculate "Net Real Gain Rate" which is the rate of annual increase in value of account when accounting for inflation. This is merely the annual rate of appreciation minus the inflation rate because inflation eats away at the growth rate.

- Calculate the "Net Nominal Gain Rate," which is the apparent dollar value of the account. This is the sum of the capital appreciation and the inflation rate, so it represents the apparent dollar increase in the account.

| Scenario | Tax Bracket | Annual Capital Gain | Annual Inflation | Net Real Gain Rate | Net Nominal Gain Rate |
|---|---|---|---|---|---|
| Very Pessimistic | 22% | -1% | 10% | -11% | 9% |
| Pessimistic | 22% | 6% | 4% | 2% | 10% |
| Average | 22% | 7% | 3% | 4% | 10% |
| Optimistic | 22% | 8% | 2% | 6% | 10% |
| Very Optimistic | 22% | 10% | 2% | 8% | 12% |

We calculate our starting principal in pre- and post-tax:

- We assume the same starting principal of $19,500 over the different scenarios.

- Pre-tax contributions aren't taxed, so the principal amount is the full amount.

- Post-tax contributions are taxed so we take net contribution as principal or 88% (i.e. 100%-22%=88%) of $19,500 which is $15,210.

| Scenario | Pre-tax Contribution Principal | Post-tax Contribution Principal |
|---|---|---|
| Very Pessimistic | $19,500 | $15,210 |
| Pessimistic | $19,500 | $15,210 |
| Average | $19,500 | $15,210 |
| Optimistic | $19,500 | $15,210 |
| Very Optimistic | $19,500 | $15,210 |

Here is what returns after withdrawal of the $19,500 under different income tax brackets.

| Scenario | Pre-Tax Real Value after 20 years | Post-Tax Real Value after 20 years | Tax Bracket % Withdrawal |
|---|---|---|---|
| Very Pessimistic | $1,895.98 | $1,440.95 | 32% |
| Pessimistic | $28,975.97 | $22,021.74 | 22% |
| Average | $42,726.90 | $32,472.44 | 22% |
| Optimistic | $62,539.14 | $47,529.75 | 12% |
| Very Optimistic | $90,888.66 | $69,075.38 | 12% |

| Scenario | Pre-Tax Real Withdrawal Amount After Taxes | Post-Tax Real Withdrawal Amount After Taxes |
|---|---|---|
| Very Pessimistic | $1,289.27 | $1,440.95 |
| Pessimistic | $22,601.26 | $22,021.74 |
| Average | $33,326.98 | $32,472.44 |
| Optimistic | $55,034.44 | $47,529.75 |
| Very Optimistic | $79,982.02 | $69,075.38 |

*Note*: from the above simulation most of the scenarios favor pre-tax contributions except for "Very Pessimistic", which has a higher withdrawal income tax and maybe unrealistic tax on withdrawal rate.

Why is it that pre-tax contributions net larger returns? Generally, the savings on pre-tax contributions means a larger principle, which can compound over time. Further, we assume that the tax withdrawal rate on retirement is lower than the tax rate during contribution. If the tax rate on contributions is the same or higher than the tax rate on withdrawals, then it's more beneficial to use the post-tax contributions.

The above tables were based on the following tax brackets as of 2023:

## Tax Brackets for Married Filed Jointly

10% for $0–20k

12% for $20k–80k

22% for $80–178k

24% for $178k–340k

32% for $340k–431k

Naturally, the question arises: can we assume that tax brackets will be relatively stable? The question of tax stability is also a bit more complicated and contentious than commonly known, as the reasons are political. For instance, some sites show that the top 1% of earners have paid nearly the same percent tax brackets but support a disproportionately large part of the tax burden in absolute dollars of the whole country.[13][14]

In the 1970s, the tax bracket for annual income >$200k was about 70%. In contrast to 2023, the tax bracket is ~32%, and the top tax bracket is 37% for incomes of greater than $578k. In the last 60 years, for 90% of the US population, rates have been relatively stable. Prior to the 1980s, the tax percentage on the top 0.01% was about 70%. Thereafter, the Top 0.1% dropped to 30%.[15]

Raw data for tax rates are here: https://taxfoundation.org/historical-income-tax-rates-brackets/.

## 1.4 Additional Thoughts on Taxes

Per Benjamin Franklin, there are only two certainties: "Death and Taxes." This section is by no means a comprehensive guide to minimizing the tax burden. An entirely separate book could be written just on this subject. Regardless, I feel obligated to include some content here about taxes and additional insights.

The main idea to those new to personal finance is that, in the U.S., we use a progressive tax system (i.e., income is taxed at different rates within "tax brackets"). What this means is that if an individual is in the 24% tax bracket, their entire income isn't taxed at that rate. Rather, the portion of their income that falls within that bracket is taxed at that rate. See the below chart:

13. Do the rich pay their fair share?. Federal Budget in Pictures. (2024, March 21). https://www.federalbudgetinpictures.com/do-the-rich-pay-their-fair-share/

14. Summary of the latest federal income tax data, 2024 update. Tax Foundation. (2024, April 2). https://taxfoundation.org/data/all/federal/latest-federal-income-tax-data-20244.

15. Chait, Jonathan. "A Peek into the Fantasy World of the Persecuted Rich." Intelligencer, 25 Sept. 2012, nymag.com/intelligencer/2012/09/fantasy-world-of-the-persecuted-rich.html.

| Tax Rate | on taxable income from ... | up to ... |
|---|---|---|
| 10 | $0 | $11,000 |
| 12 | $11,001 | $44,725 |
| 22 | $44,726 | $95,375 |
| 24 | $95,376 | $182,100 |
| 32 | $182,101 | $231,250 |
| 35 | $231,251 | $578,125 |
| 37 | $578,126 | And up |

Source: https://www.irs.gov/filing/federal-income-tax-rates-and-brackets

For example, if an individual is making $100,000/year then the first ~$11,000 is taxed at 10% and then their income from $11,001 to $44,725 is taxed at 12% etc.

**Dividends and Interest are Taxed as Ordinary Income**
Many folks make it a game to hunt around for the highest-yielding savings account or collect high dividend securities. Nothing wrong with earning risk-free income with the caveat it might be kicking an individual into a higher tax bracket as interest and dividends are taxed as ordinary income.

Companies that pay dividends do so at the opportunity cost of reinvestment in their business. This can act as a double tax in the sense that the company is paying some percent of its earnings to a dividend, and the stock's owners pay a tax on the income from that dividend. This is evidenced by the fact that the market cap (the total value of its outstanding stocks) decreases by the total dividend paid. The alternative to paying a dividend is for the company to reinvest its capital. This means that a) the stock retains the value of the dividend, and b) the investor doesn't pay any taxes on the dividend.

Lastly, interest is often not paid at much higher than the current fed fund rate and probably not significantly more than inflation (though 2022/2023 is a weird time). I think it only makes sense to search for these investments/savings accounts in the absence of alternative investment activities.

### 1031 Real Estate Rule

The number "1031" is incidentally the NCC number of the starship *Discovery* in the eponymous Star Trek show, but the rule itself is, unfortunately, about something far more mundane. The basic idea is that a 1031 exchange is a swap of a real estate investment property for another that allows taxes on real estate sale gains to be deferred. A savvy real estate investor can avoid paying taxes on real estate gains and accumulate significant wealth. The rules and qualifications for this are quite complex, so it is necessary to consult an expert in this field before attempting to do this. Mainly, this is an important tip to include because of its relationship to a critical cultural franchise and treasure.

## Summary

In this chapter, we explored the main retirement questions: "How much do I need to retire? And when?". To answer these questions, we need to decompose the problem into sub-questions such as, "What are my annual expenses?" and "What are my sources of debt?"

We described a few ways of tracking expenses such as YNAB and reviewed different types of accounts. Among these account types, we specifically examined the difference between Pre-tax and Post-tax retirement accounts, and how to contribute to them and in what order.

Lastly, we covered some ideas to guide reducing the tax burden.

This chapter is intended as a conceptual foundation upon which we will build our plans for investment portfolios. The construction of that portfolio is the subject of Chapter 2!

# Chapter 2: Portfolio Construction

The basic idea of portfolio construction is to maximize return and minimize risk through diversification via uncorrelated asset selection. In *Pioneering Portfolio Management*, Swensen refers to this as mean variance optimization, which is a fancy way of saying picking assets that are uncorrelated and have low variance (volatility) but high upside.[1] We'll discuss risk and expected value in greater detail in another section.

Portfolio construction is similar to the knapsack problem[2][3] in computer science where the goal is to fill said knapsack with objects to maximize value. Each potential object has some cost (e.g., volume) to be added to the knapsack and some value. This problem is considered to be computationally expensive (i.e., "NP Complete" in computer science parlance).

## 2.1 Asset Classes

It's hard to have a discussion about portfolio construction without a discussion of the possible component asset classes. However, this tends to be a tedious rehashing of their definitions, so I'll just give a brief description and discuss only the more interesting aspects of a particular asset class and leave the basics to the reader as additional investigation.

---

1. Swensen, David F. Pioneering portfolio management: An unconventional approach to institutional investment, fully revised and updated. Simon and Schuster, 2009.

2. https://en.wikipedia.org/wiki/Knapsack_problem

3. Mathews, George B. "On the partition of numbers." Proceedings of the London Mathematical Society 1.1 (1896): 486-490.

### Fixed Income (Bonds, CD, Treasuries)

This is usually considered the low-risk portion of a portfolio, so it should only include high-quality fixed income. For example, a corporate bond, while it may have a higher return, generally has about the same downside risk as its corresponding equity. For example, if the probability of a company failing in the next year is 10%, then the bond has a 10% chance of not being paid back. Whereas equity with the same probability of going to zero (10%) has a much higher upside compared to the bond, which has only its interest payments.

Treasuries, on the other hand, have the probability of not being paid back at about the same probability of the U.S. not paying its debt down. The U.S. government not paying its debt isn't an impossible event – it is just a much lower probability than a company going bankrupt.

CDs are another good choice, but take care to pick FDIC-insured CDs in the event a bank fails. Keep in mind that several decades ago we had about 10,000 banks – presently there are about 4,000–5,000 banks in the U.S. So bank failure, while low probability, isn't risk free.

TIPS (Treasury Inflation Protected Securities) would also fall into the fixed-income asset class. These are supposed to protect assets against unexpected inflation. This is probably fine if held over the long run, but when the fed rate rises above the TIP rate, expect a drop in extrinsic value.

The extrinsic value of the bond is the price for which the bond can be sold in the open market. The extrinsic value varies depending on the interest rate environment. If the bond interest rate is high in a low interest rate environment, then the bond is worth more compared to similar bonds but of a lower interest rate, e.g., a bond from company A has an interest rate of 5% in 2023 and company A offers a bond for 3% in 2024: then, of course, the bond from 2023 is worth more.

### Commodities

Commodities include precious metals, oil, agriculture, etc. Generally, folks buy commodities for two reasons:

1. the possibility of a ton of money out of knowledge asymmetry

2. a hedge against inflation.

There are at least a couple of ways to invest in commodities: either through an ETF or by buying the commodity straight out. Purchasing commodity futures is also a possibility, but we leave that for serious investing professionals.

For commodity investors, the custody of assets may be handed over to third parties (usually at a high fee level). Where significant amounts of a commodity are purchased, questions such as on-site security, geographical diversification, insurance, and management become important. On the other hand, investing in an ETF has other risks, such as the actual asset may not be in the actual custody of the ETF management itself. In the event of a crisis, it can be questionable if the ETF is actually worth the paper it claims to hold.

### ETF vs index funds:

Since the rise in popularity of passive investing, many investment companies have started to put out low-quality ETFs with high fees. More perniciously, these fees are generally flat fees applied to the fund regardless of performance. This is money that the unwary purchaser is simply giving away to fund managers. One might argue that, as long as the fund does well, then that fee pays for itself – this is a reasonable position, but it supports a culture of low-quality investment products coupled with fleecing the consumer. It's up to the consumer to decide if this is a cost worth paying. On the other hand, index funds offer much lower fees. Vanguard generally has low fees and well-constructed funds.

### Real Estate

Real estate performance is highly dependent on the local market (i.e., some areas of the U.S. do very well, while others do not). If an individual grew up in an area where real estate did well, they probably have relatives and friends espousing the financial rewards of such an investment. Such advice should be balanced by a couple of facts. Firstly, national real estate, on average, has had a real return of about only 1% per year since the 1960s.

Secondly, there are understated costs of owning real estate. For example:

- cost of capital (mortgage interest payments)

- property taxes

- maintenance costs

- property management (if the intent is renting)

- opportunity costs, e.g., an index fund that does 6–8% annually

Note: the down payment isn't considered part of the cost because its value is considered part of the equity in the home.

A 5% annual unrecoverable cost of home ownership is a good conservative heuristic to use when considering the total cost of ownership. Additionally, real estate is not as fungible (easily converted to cash) as other types of assets (i.e., a property may sit on the market for months or years). Additionally, a sale may mean large tax on the asset.

For most Americans, a primary residence already represents a substantial proportion of their net worth. It's worth thinking critically whether the further concentration of assets is worth the opportunity cost vs. diversification into other asset classes. While there are certainly opportunities in the real estate market, another consideration is that a casual investor is competing against other real estate and property management companies that do this full-time. For the casual investor, there may be other more liquid and easier alternative investments, such as Real Estate Investment Trusts (REITs).

### REITs

REITs offer exposure to real estate in a diversified manner, with fees and composition similar to ETF and index funds, and there's a similar level of liquidity (i.e., one can sell REITs quickly within a few days compared to months to years to sell a house). Also, REITs may be protected from geographical risk through diversification (verification of this diversification should be part of good due diligence). The risk level is generally considered to be between that of fixed income/bonds and index funds. Real estate, in general, has historically acted as a good hedge against inflation.

### Crypto

Crypto might be considered as any asset that is secured using blockchain technology. Crypto is a diverse and quickly evolving asset class. It is also one fraught with misinformation (accidental spread of erroneous information), disinformation (intentional spread of erroneous information), scandal, scams, and simple misunderstanding. See the Appendix for further discussion. This section will only give a surface-level introduction to this asset class (it could be an entirely separate book in its own right), so it's contingent upon the reader to do a deep dive to truly understand the subject.

What is crypto? Cryptocurrencies originated with Bitcoin and the famous Satoshi white paper on the subject. It's called *crypto* because cryptographic algorithms are used to verify and secure transactions on a virtual ledger and *hashed*. Hashing is an algorithm that outputs a collision-resistant numeric value from its input, or, in other words, a different input should yield a unique output. The same input will always yield the same output value. A *cryptographic hash* is a hashing algorithm that is extremely difficult to reverse, i.e., given the output number to determine what was the input value. In fact, the only way to reasonably accomplish finding the original input is to guess a bunch of inputs and see if the hashed value matches the desired output value. In order to verify transactions on the blockchain, a network of computers is constantly trying to guess/calculate these input hashes. A computer on the chain that correctly guesses/calculates the input hash will successfully prove that it's done the work to verify the transactions on the chain, i.e., proof of work. This result is verified by the other nodes on the network, whereupon a consensus is reached that, indeed, the transaction was successful. Different crypto networks use different algorithms/schemes to accomplish validation of transactions on the network and secure it against fraudulent transactions.

The crypto ecosystem is a large subject that is continuously evolving. There are, of course, scams, but there are also crypto-currencies that might be considered akin to "blue chip" stocks – e.g., Bitcoin (BTC), Ethereum (ETH), or Solana (SOL). The currencies have, in the portfolio theory parlance, "high variance," i.e., price action can be as much as a couple of standard deviations in both directions. However, these higher-quality cryptocurrencies have shown to hold their value relatively well over the years. Other types of coins include stable coins (such as USDC) and mixers (such as Monero) that provide anonymity. Yet another class of coins provides analytics to the crypto community (e.g., GRT) and solves problems such as getting real-world data onto the blockchain (e.g., Link) and providing blockchain storage (e.g., Filecoin or Arweave). Most recently, the trend in crypto projects to run code on blockchain networks (called Smart Contracts) has significant implications for the shape of the tech world in the coming years.

Despite myriad potential risks, crypto ought to now be considered a mainstream asset for several reasons. Firstly, BTC has been around for more than 14 years. Secondly, you are required to pay taxes on crypto investment profits.

In assessing the value of these blockchain networks, one shouldn't observe just the price action of the security but rather the group of developers toiling tirelessly to innovate and develop these networks. Investing in what is termed "long tail strategy" is the idea of making several high-risk investments with the expectation of a very few making large returns that more than make up for the majority of failed investments. This is a similar strategy in the venture capital (VC) world. VC makes a good comparison because investment in a particular coin is really investing in the network of developers supporting a crypto project and also because of the degree of innovation and the likelihood of significant industry disruption.

In general, crypto is a highly volatile asset class that is starting to see increased legitimacy through taxes, government regulation/laws, adoption, and financial investment products. There are significant risks, and it's up to the investor to do adequate due diligence and decide if it ought to be considered part of their portfolio.

## 2.2 Choosing Portfolio Components

In order to get the benefits of risk mitigation through diversification, one ought to choose asset classes that don't strongly correlate with each other. For example, picking both growth and value stocks often has a high correlation – the implication being that if one declines in value, so will the other. One of the major problems in picking equities is their high correlation to each other. Simply picking a broad index fund doesn't achieve risk reduction through diversification if all the stocks in that fund are highly correlated.

It's important to diversify across different asset classes. For a long time, the 60/40 asset allocation split was the de facto standard as the equities were inversely correlated to bonds. In different macroeconomic environments, this is not always a safe assumption. Adding other types of assets can help mitigate macro risks in a particular asset class.

Swensen advocates being cautious about what asset classes to add to a portfolio that may add more risk without significantly better upside.[4] An example, as discussed above, is adding corporate bonds with a slightly higher yield but not the same upside as simply purchasing the company's stock.

---

4. Swensen, David F. *Pioneering portfolio management: An unconventional approach to institutional investment, fully revised and updated.* Simon and Schuster, 2009.

### Choosing Allocation Sizes

The basic rule of thumb in Swensen,[5] Graham,[6] and Dalio[7] is to allocate no less than 5–10% to an asset class because any smaller amount won't have a material effect on a portfolio's outcomes. Similarly, no more than 30–40% should be allocated to a single asset class because it overweights the portfolio and decreases benefits of risk mitigation via diversification.

### Passive Investing

Passive investing is basically the idea of simply adding a fixed amount to a particular asset, usually an index fund at periodic intervals over a longer period of time.

## 2.3 Examples of Portfolio Allocations

In this section, we explore some possible portfolio allocations that the reader can use as a starting point that could be applied to their own portfolio allocations (with proper amount of due diligence). These aren't recommendations, as each person's financial requirements differ in at least the following significant ways:

- assets available for investment

- appetite for risk

- time horizon for investment

- investment goals

We start first with David Swensen's *Pioneering portfolio management*,[8] which discusses the investment philosophy of Yale's endowment fund. David

---

5. Swensen, David F. *Unconventional success: A fundamental approach to personal investment.* Simon and Schuster, 2005.

6. Graham, Benjamin, and Luke Daniels. *The Intelligent Investor* rev ed. HarperCollins, 2015.

7. Dalio, Ray. *Principles.* Simon and Schuster, 2018.

8. Swensen, David F. *Pioneering portfolio management: An unconventional approach to institutional investment,* fully revised and updated. Simon and Schuster, 2009.

Swensen was from 1985 to 2021 the chief investment officer of Yale, where it went from $1bn to a 2019 total of $29.4bn:

- U.S. equity: 12%

- U.S. bonds: 4%

- foreign equity: 15%

- private equity (investment in private companies): 17%

- absolute return (event/value-driven strategies): 25%

- real assets: 27%

- cash: 0

Yale's endowment fund has a well-funded team of investment professionals that has resources and time to devote to more specialized assets and investment strategies, such as private equity and absolute return. Private equity is an investment in private companies. Absolute return is an investment that takes advantage of particular events, such as mergers and acquisitions or value strategies that attempt to generate profit from mispricings and/or the use of options to offset risk.

This brings us to the important points of difference between use cases for different portfolios. Most casual (retail) investors do not have the equivalent time and resources to invest the same way an established institution does. Consider someone who does a day job casually a couple hours a day vs. someone doing it full time every day. Further, consider what could be accomplished if there's an entire team of specialists who have deep experience/education/knowledge/connections in these areas doing this activity every day.

In contrast, in Swensen's *Unconventional success*,[9] he recommends a considerably different allocation:

- domestic equity: 30%

---

9. Swensen, David F. *Unconventional success: A fundamental approach to personal investment.* Simon and Schuster, 2005.

- foreign equity: 15%

- emerging market equity: 5%

- U.S. Treasury bonds: 15%

- U.S. TIPS: 15%

Note the omission of private equity and absolute return and the replacement of U.S. bonds with U.S. treasury bonds. This is probably done to offset the knowledge requirement to invest properly in U.S. bonds with an equivalent asset class of similar volatility but requiring less research and management, i.e., treasury bonds.

### Warren Buffett Portfolio Allocation

Does Warren Buffet, the oracle of Omaha, with a net worth of $120bn really need an introduction?

- U.S. stocks: 90%

- fixed income: 10%

This is a hero allocation – no normal person ought to have this allocation as its risk profile is considerably higher than most non-professional investors ought to accept.

### Kristy Shen's Quit Like a Millionaire Portfolio

Kristy Shen started her journey to FIRE with a story about digging through garbage in China as a child, and hit her "number" at 31 and quit her job to travel. She writes about her retirement/investing journey in her book *Quit like a millionaire*.[10]

- Bonds: 40%

  o government: 10%

  o corporate: 10%

---

10. Shen, Kristy, and Bryce Leung. *Quit like a millionaire: no gimmicks, luck, or trust fund required*. Penguin, 2019.

- o preferred: 20%

- U.S. index: 30%

  - o S&P: 15%

  - o REITs: 10%

  - o dividend stocks: 5%

- EAFE index (foreign equity): 30%

This portfolio allocation is skewed towards heavier dividend/yield as opposed to asset price appreciation. If an individual is retired, as in the case of Kristy Shen, it's nice to have a regular income with relatively low risk. Dividends are taxed as ordinary income, so it might make less sense if an individual has regular income and is trying to stay below a certain tax bracket. In the context of minimizing risk, my personal opinion is that adding corporate bonds only increases risk with only a slight increase in yield. Similarly, the inclusion of REITs in U.S. equity skews towards less risk than pure equity exposure.

Kristy Shen's portfolio highlights an important point. Where a person is in their life affects their financial allocation choices. In the case of Kristy Shen, having achieved financial independence, her allocation choices skew towards receiving income. Further, depending on a person's "number," they may decide that any excess amount might be better served in higher risk/return bets. For example, if an individual knows they need $2m to last the remainder of their life in a comfortable lifestyle and they actually have $2.2m (an excess of $200k), they could comfortably allocate $200k to a high-risk asset like crypto and the remaining $2m into something lower risk like fixed income.

### Ray Dalio All Weather Portfolio
Ray Dalio (net worth $19.1bn) is known for his association with Bridgewater Associates.

- SPY (ETF for S&P 500): 30%

- long-term bonds: 40%

- intermediate U.S. bonds: 15%

- gold: 7.5%

- commodities: 7.5%

This seems like a good diversification across different asset classes that has good risk mitigation by choosing asset classes that historically have been fairly decoupled from each other.

### Chris Camilo's Lockbox and Big Money Portfolio

Chris Camilo, featured in Jack Schwager's *Unknown Market Wizards,*[11] took $84,000 and turned it into $42m in 15 years. Chris Camilo follows a slightly different approach to portfolio allocation as outlined in his book *Laughing at Wall Street.*[12] Having achieved his retirement "number," he keeps a portion of his assets in what he calls his "lockbox" account – investments in relatively low risk to maintain long-term financial security. The rest of his assets are placed in what he terms an "other people's money" (OPM) or "big money" account. This big money account is what he uses to make higher risk/return investments. It is because of this compartmentalization of assets between low-risk and high-risk that he is able to psychologically take the high-risk/return investments. It's not unusual for him to put as much as 50% of his big money account into a single investment.

## 2.4 Implementing Your Personal Portfolio

There are many models and advice on picking a portfolio allocation, so the challenge is to pick an allocation that aligns rationally with lifestyle, appetite for risk, and financial needs. The point here is not to advocate for a particular portfolio allocation but to give you a rough framework with which to design and critique your portfolio allocation. As Swensen points out, picking a well-reasoned portfolio distribution and having the discipline to stick to it was a major factor in Yale's endowments' enduring success.

If you're not comfortable picking an allocation or have limited experience or confidence you can examine how much risk you're willing to take and

---

11. Schwager, Jack D. *Unknown market wizards: The best traders you've never heard of.* Harriman House Limited, 2020.

12. Camillo, Chris. *Laughing at Wall Street: How I beat the pros at investing (by reading tabloids, shopping at the mall, and connecting on Facebook) and how you can, too.* St Martin's Press, 2011.

select one of the allocations from above (e.g. Ray Dalio's All Weather Portfolio) and tune it over time as your knowledge and appetite for risk changes over time.

It's my opinion that it's necessary for owners of a portfolio distribution to come to these reasoned conclusions rather than blindly accepting a particular allocation from various influencers. Conviction in one's choices must be grown in parallel with an investor's appetite for risk over time. This is the difference between an experienced investor and a new one. In times of duress – say several years of a recession – an investor will fail to invest in what is apparent losing investments and similarly fail to sell investments doing well. Such an investor falls into the familiar fallacy of selling low and buying high rather than the opposite, buying low and selling high.

To assist with keeping your discipline:

1. State the desired portfolio allocation on paper in the form of a personal investment agreement with yourself. Larry Swedroe, in *Think, Act, and Invest Like Warren Buffett*,[13] recommends writing an "investment policy statement" (i.e., a statement of investment intent) and then signing it.

2. Start a log/journal listing the reasons why you chose those particular allocations.

For (2), it's important to record your thoughts/reasons at the point you made those decisions so you can reflect on them later. Even if it's the statement: "I chose 60/40% U.S. equities/bonds because I read it in a book or online."

## Summary

In this chapter, we covered basic ideas behind portfolio construction to reduce risk via diversification across different asset classes. Merely having distinct assets yields no risk mitigation if the underlying assets are highly correlated. So we included a brief discussion of the different asset classes.

We then examined different portfolio allocations from different investors and compared and contrasted their portfolio styles and risks.

Finally, we explored concrete ways of implementing our own portfolio.

---

13. Swedroe, Larry. *Think, act, and invest like Warren Buffett*. McGraw-Hill Education, 2012.

# Chapter 3: Essentials of Investing

Many of the subjects in this chapter are complex enough to be their own book or even college course by themselves. The point of this chapter is to give an overview from which a reader can start their own investigations.

## 3.1 Risk and Expected Value

In regard to basic probability, Charlie Munger (investor/philanthropist with a net worth of $2.6bn) put it eloquently: "If you don't get [...] elementary probability, then you go through a long life like a one-legged man in an ass-kicking contest."[1]

Most folk think of risk in terms of "How much can I lose?" So, risk is framed in terms of a loss. While losing one's investment is certainly undesirable, this definition is problematic for a few reasons:

1. It's imprecise in that it's difficult to quantify risk in a meaningful sense. Does it mean one could lose an entire investment or just a portion? What is the likelihood of this loss? How can we compare one "risky" investment to another alternative investment?

2. It is too easy to fall into the psychological fallacy of loss aversion (i.e., an unwary investor can incorrectly focus attention on losses to the exclusion of gains).

A better conceptual model for measuring risk is the statistical definition of expected value or the probability of a loss multiplied by the amount at stake:

**Risk = Expected Value of Loss = Probability of Loss * Amount at Stake**

1. Munger, Charlie. "A lesson on elementary worldly wisdom." Address to the University of Southern California Marshall School of Business (1994).

This definition accounts for (1) the likelihood of loss, (2) the value at stake, and (3) gives a metric that can be compared between two potential investments.

*Example*: If I think there is a 9 out of 10 chance (90% probability) of losing the entire investment of $1000, then my expected value on that investment is $100. Or, in terms of loss, an expected loss of $900.

While it can be difficult to calculate exactly the probability of loss, we can limit the amount at stake to a large loss potential. As alluded to above, we're missing a key component to this calculation, which is the upside or gain from the investment. We can calculate this gain in a similar way as calculating loss (i.e., probability of gain * how much can be gained).

*Example*: if there's a 1 out of 10 chance of $1000 turning into $100,000, then the expected value is $10,000 because (1/10) * $100,000 = $10,000.

Combining the expected value of the loss with the expected value of the gain is simply the sum of the two expected values for gain and loss, respectively.

In the above example, we had an expected value gain of $10,000 and an expected value loss of -$900. We just sum these values as below:

$10,000 – $900 = $9,100

Is this a good investment? $9100 is more than 9x the initial investment of $1000. Another interpretation is a bet on such odds over multiple bets will, on average, return 9x the original stake amount. 9/10 times, you would lose most of the initial investment, but 1/10 times, you would make $100,000. Given a single bet, most folk focus on losing the 9/10 times, losing 90% of their investment. The phenomenon of focusing on the loss of investment without including the upside gain is called loss aversion.

The anticipated pain from loss aversion is a strong disincentive against making such an investment. In this case, loss aversion leads to an irrational decision to avoid the potential of pain from loss, despite the mathematically sound choice to make the bet because the average outcome is greater than zero. In *Thinking, fast and slow* Daniel Kahneman explores the various mental flaws associated with loss aversion that explains the exclusion of the beneficial side of the equation.[2] We'll discuss other mental fallacies that can affect judgment and different mechanisms/techniques to overcome these all-too-human instincts in a later section.

### Assigning Probability and Volatility (Beta)

Calculating expected value is a good approach to rationally assessing risk/reward. However, in practice, it's difficult to assign an actual probability to certain events. We could approach a given asset and calculate statistically its variability from its historical data. This is certainly a valid approach to assessing how much the price will vary over time. In modern portfolio theory, this variability is referred to as volatility. Using the past history of an asset, such as stock price, we can calculate how large its standard deviation is (i.e., some stocks have a wider standard deviation and, therefore, vary widely in their price).

A caveat about calculating stock prices: a feature of stock prices is that their price action is non-stationary (i.e. the mean and standard deviation changes over time) and has a positive bias (i.e. the stock market has a tendency to go up).

This statistical perspective on risk gave rise to the risk metric of beta (i.e., how much of a portfolio's risk is correlated with the market).

- beta = 1: target portfolio has the same risk as the market

- beta > 1: target portfolio has a greater risk than the market

- beta < 1: target portfolio has a lesser risk than the market

For example, a portfolio with a beta == 2 means that it will swing twice as much as the market. Similarly, a portfolio with a beta == 0.5 means that it will swing about half as much as the market.

The use of beta in constructing low beta, high return portfolios is known as the capital-asset pricing model (CAPM). If the savvy investor can achieve the same return for lower volatility, then it is the more desirable investment. Seasoned investors use backwards looking indicators, such as historical beta, as a guidepost and are accordingly cognizant that past behavior isn't a guarantee of future performance.

So, how can we quantify the probability? In our analysis of a particular investment, we can draw on a variety of different sources:

---

2. Kahneman, Daniel. *Thinking, fast and slow.* Macmillan, 2011.

- Examine past price action: this can give some indication as to how much volatility an asset has or equivalently how much of a drawdown has occurred in the past.

- Examine the behavior of similar investments and markets.

- Use a qualitative measure (e.g., a high probability of failure when investing in a friend's questionable NFT startup).

- Use fermi-ization (discussed later) to estimate the probability relative to other investments.

**Mitigating Risk**

There are many strategies for mitigating risk, and each has its negatives/positives. Some trading risk-mitigation techniques include the following:

- using stop-loss orders to prevent large movements in price action from taking out an investment position

- using options to straddle a particular price

- investing less if the market goes against the original expectation

- limiting the amount of risk capital.

For most retail investors, risk mitigation in the form of asset class diversification is the lowest-maintenance approach. In asset diversification, the goal is to achieve mean-variance optimization (i.e., maximizing return and minimizing risk). Further understanding beyond the basics requires a dive into modern portfolio theory, but we won't delve into it here as these specifics are too detailed and out of scope.

*Note*: More advanced investors will dynamically rebalance and allocate in reaction to changes in macro and market conditions.

This is contrary to common wisdom, which says something like 70% of active management funds fail to beat the index. That means there's still 30% of the managers who beat the market. We also know from work done in Superforecasters[3] that about 1–2% of the population can consistently make

---

3. Tetlock, Philip E., and Dan Gardner. Superforecasting: The Art and Science of Prediction. Random House Business, 2019.

successful predictions. Even teams of non-superforecasters improved their accuracy by 23% over individuals. So, it's a little irrational to accept the conclusion that active management can't be successful.

Oftentimes (but not always) high reward investment opportunities go hand in hand with high risk (high probability of failure). Pragmatically, if a high-risk/reward investment is desired, it might make sense to segregate these investments from a mean variance optimized (i.e. diversified) portfolio. This will prevent the investor from physically mixing investing strategies and unintentionally increasing risk within the carefully diversified portfolio.

Due diligence is another way of qualitatively mitigating risk, which we'll discuss in another section.

## 3.2 Efficient Market Hypothesis

Before discussing due diligence, the idea of efficient market hypothesis (EMH, not to be confused with the more commonly used term "Emergency Medical Hologram")[4] must be introduced and critiqued because of the implications of research/investigation on an investment thesis. EMH is the idea that the price of the stock reflects all the possible information that can be obtained, and market participants have voted rationally by paying fair market value for an asset. The implication is that it's impossible to gain alpha (advantage) through having superior investment knowledge. If EMH is true, it obviates the point of doing investigation/research. However, EMH is problematic for several reasons.

Firstly, there exists a set of market participants (e.g., "market wizards")[5] who consistently beat the market and continue to beat the market beyond what statistics and survivorship bias would suggest. There are individuals in every field who perform 10x better than the majority in accordance with power law distribution. This is consistent with findings in the book *Superforecasters* where the top 2% of forecasters have superior and consistent forecasts. There are specific characteristics these individuals tend to display, which correlate with success in investing and forecasting, such as open mindedness, discipline, higher than average education/intelligence, a tendency towards numeracy and probabilistic proficiency, etc. Further, they

---

4. https://memory-alpha.fandom.com/wiki/Emergency_Medical_Holographic_program

5. Schwager, Jack D. *Market Wizards, Updated: Interviews with Top Traders.* John Wiley & Sons, 2012.

tend to develop specific trading/forecasting systems that use feedback loops to systematically improve over time.

Secondly, beating the market can be engineered, as in the case of Yale endowment fund management and the Bridgewater hedge fund. Swensen credits Yale endowment fund success to keeping discipline with predetermined portfolio allocations for obviating risk by rebalancing overweight allocations into underweight allocations. Bridgewater, under Ray Dalio, operates in accordance with principles outlined in his book Principles, a set of guidelines for operating and making investment decisions. As a side note, many of the "principles" he outlines mitigate many of the mental judgment fallacies in Daniel Kahneman's *Thinking, fast and slow*.

Thirdly, there are large variations in the distribution of market knowledge. Compare the knowledge asymmetry between a retail investor and a seasoned analyst. It's hard to argue that they're both making investing decisions based on the same information set. Traders like Chris Carmelo of Dumb Money use social arbitrage to gain alpha and use techniques such as sentiment detection that are hardly accessible to the average Robinhood ape. Further, trading is often a psychological exercise rather than a problem of determining purely value propositions.

Lastly, some markets/investments are more efficient than others (i.e., market knowledge is more evenly distributed). Incentives of large institutions differ from retail investors in that retaining clients and capital preservations lead to different operating behaviors and choices of investments that tend towards more conservative bets rather than high risk/high reward. This is related to the number of industry analysts that focus on large, commonly traded securities vs. smaller, less frequently traded securities. The implication is that alpha is more likely in investments where efficiency is low (i.e., market knowledge is asymmetrically distributed). Even in highly efficient markets, such as energy and commodities, where the supply and consumption ought to be predictable with high seasonality, it's possible to gain alpha.

EMH ought to be used as a descriptor for how much information is evenly distributed. Certain markets can be described as more efficient than others. However, EMH can't be taken as a truism for the reasons listed above.

Philosophically, if we accepted EMH as true, what would be the point/fun in investing if it were impossible to beat the market?

## 3.3 Opportunity Cost

Opportunity cost is the cost of the road not taken. For example, suppose we have $100, and we only have two choices:

1. invest in a CD making 5% or
2. invest in stock, earning 8% per year.

If we chose 1 (a CD at 5%/year) our opportunity cost is what we would've earned had we invested in the stock at 8% – a difference of 3%. So, the opportunity cost is 3% or $3.

One might argue that if we have already chosen the CD, then the alternative stock doesn't exist and isn't a real choice. Of course, once we've made a choice, and unless we're a time-traveling doctor in a box[6] or in possession of a Delorean retrofitted with an operational flux capacitor,[7] we can't go back and remake the same choice.

The concept of opportunity cost is best applied in a forward-looking context when confronted with a series of different choices and considering whether to commit to a specific choice at the cost of the alternatives. We gave a brief outline of expected value in prior chapters as a tool to compare two or more investments in a numerical way.

## 3.4 Due Diligence

Not doing due diligence is like playing poker without looking at one's hand. It's our responsibility to verify the essential points of any investment thesis. After all, it is our own money, and whether we've made a bad gamble or not is based on our decisions. Even if we've been misled, to a certain extent, we've allowed ourselves to be duped into an incorrect position. Due diligence can take many forms, and different investment practitioners approach doing

---

6. https://en.wikipedia.org/wiki/Doctor_Who

7. https://en.wikipedia.org/wiki/Back_to_the_Future

due diligence in different ways. For this section, we'll focus primarily on stock as the main vehicle of investment, as it represents the asset class most retail/casual investors are familiar with.

All publicly traded companies are required by the SEC (Security and Exchange Commission) to publish their financials in accordance with GAAP (Generally Accepted Accounting Principles). GAAP sets out definitions and accounting rules for publishing financial information for a given company. The main financial statements are the income statement, balance sheet, and cash flow. It can take time to learn how to read and interpret these documents. As discussed in the *Efficient Market Hypothesis* section, keep in mind that all of this information is public, and we're unlikely to develop a significant edge. What we *can* do is verify certain statements such as "x company's annual revenue has doubled in the last year" or "Is this company solvent?" The full scope of reading financial statements is probably an entire accounting class on its own, so we'll focus on only a few parts to give you a general idea.

**Income Statement**

The income statement is an overview of how much money the company makes, broken down by revenue and operating expenses. Net income is "revenue" less "expenses.

**Balance Sheet**

- assets = what the company owns, e.g. inventory

- liabilities = debts

- equity = assets – liabilities. Equity is sometimes interpreted as how much the company is worth.

**Cash Flow**

The cash flow is an overview of how money was spent and brought in:

- cash from operations: money generated from the normal operating of the company (e.g., sales);

- cash from investing: money made from selling securities;

- cash from financing: any loans taken out.

From this minimal set, we should be able to determine the following:

- Is the company solvent? Are their assets greater than their liabilities?

- Are they making money from their core business vs. from external investment?

- Are they growing their core business or is it declining in revenue?

We may not be able to get all the answers needed from just financial statements since business is complex. A company like Amazon had negative net income for years before becoming so strongly positive. Similarly, many startups may have negative income for years as they establish their customer base. Or a large acquisition may cause a company's cash reserves to be low. Financial statements are a common reference point between two companies but are only a starting point to begin analysis. It takes time and experience to get comfortable reading financial statements, but it's well worth being literate in terminology and business.

As with most research activities, we should ask ourselves questions and then try to find the answers. Most often, a quick Google search will reveal the answer. Or sometimes it's helpful to listen in on earnings calls or read accompanying statements about the state of the business. Keep in mind all this information is public, so while an understanding of a company's public financial statements is essential, it's unlikely to give the savvy investor much edge except when compared to the casual retail investor who fails to do adequate due diligence.

## 3.5 Sanity Checks on Valuation

### P/E Ratio

The price-to-earnings (P/E) ratio is the ratio of the current price of a share to its earnings per share. Among other pricing heuristics, it has risen to prominence from Robert Shiller's book *Irrational Exuberance*,[8] where he uses it as an argument for an overpriced S&P. Intuitively, when applied to an individual company, it can be thought of as the number of earning cycles (usually years) for the aggregate earnings to be equivalent to the share price.

*Example*: a company with a P/E of 5 has a price of 5x its earnings per year.

---

8. Shiller, 8. Robert J. *Irrational exuberance*. Princeton university press, 2015.

Then, in order for a company to be valued at 5x its earnings, we'd expect it to be around for at least five years. If we predict the company to be around for ten years, then this is a pretty good deal. If we expect the company to earn substantially less or be gone in fewer than five years, then it is not a good deal. At the time of this writing, most stocks are trading with a P/E in excess of 10x and some of the most popular companies in excess of 20x. A famous chipmaker is trading, as of 2023, at a P/E of 55, which can be interpreted as its price being 55 years of earnings.

### Market Cap

Another quick due diligence step is to look at the market cap of an investment. Too many neophytes to investing/trading look at the price action of a security and use that as an indicator as to the value of a company or "how well the stock is doing." The market cap is the price times the total number of outstanding shares that are trading. Phrased another way: the total price of a particular company in the stock market. Comparing companies of similar market caps gives us a quick check to see if the price of a particular investment matches its apparent value.

*Example 1:* Let's take two companies in distinct markets and compare their market caps and their apparent value from only a few known facts. Suppose we're investigating buying TSM (Taiwan Semiconductor Mfg Company). It has a market cap of $459bn as of July 2023. We did a little research and discovered that TSM has 60% of the global market share for chip manufacturing. Suppose we don't know much about chip manufacturing, but we are familiar with the e-commerce giant Amazon, which has a market cap of $1.33tn. Amazon has about 37% of the U.S. e-commerce market. Without any more information, we can tell that both of these companies are massive conglomerates that hold huge market shares, so the apparent value must be massive. Similarly, their market caps, or what the stock market is pricing the asset at, must be similarly large. So TSM having a market cap of about a third of Amazon's seems at least in the ballpark and maybe a little underpriced as TSM's market share is global vs. Amazon's market share is only U.S. To be really sure, we'd look at TSM's market cap relative to other chip manufacturers, but that's left as an exercise for the reader.

*Example 2:* Let's consider an investment in the crypto token GRT, also known as The Graph. It indexes information about different blockchains and currently has an annual income of $127,000 and a market cap of $1.5bn at the time of this writing. At its present income rate, it would take 11,000 years to be worth its market cap. Let's compare that to Yellow Cake PLC, which has a market cap of $1.19bn and has physical holdings of uranium at secure sites – a commodity critical to nuclear power generation. Does GRT seem appropriately priced? It would seem GRT is grossly overvalued. GRT is a contrived crypto token without a proven utility in a speculative market, and YCA is a holding company for a valued commodity. Valuation of disruptive technologies often includes the effect of the anticipated disruption, which is how it can have such a high market cap.

In both examples, I used contrasting investments in totally different industries to illustrate a method of valuation between two investments. As more due diligence is done, comparisons within the same industry make more sense and finer grain comparisons can be made. For example, it makes more sense to compare TSM to INTC (Intel), AMD, or Samsung. Or GRT to BTC (Bitcoin) or ETH(Ethereum).

## Misinformation and Critical Thinking

One of the lessons I've learned in my investing journey is the prevalence of misinformation or at least information that has an agenda. Many news articles are optimized for views instead of content. We've all heard of the alleged demise of newspapers and mainstream media. In order to retain an audience, news organizations (both printed and live media forms) choose content that is light on fact and heavy on outrage. Even the facts are usually cherry-picked to support a particular narrative.

As generative AIs become more powerful, generated fake news is now indistinguishable from the human authors. Even human authors are using generative AIs to augment their writing. There is some hope: there is evidence that generative writing carries certain detectable signatures.

Even before generative AIs, in 2019, a paper called "Defending Against Neural Fake News" demonstrated the capability of neural networks to detect generated fake news.[9] My experiments in neural networks also yielded detectable differences between left- and right-leaning news sources with as high as 97% accuracy. As fake news tends to be promulgated more effectively in right-leaning social networks, it stands to reason that fake news would also contain detectable signatures. Interestingly, while we as a society have the ability to combat fake news,

---

9. Zellers, Rowan, et al. "Defending against neural fake news." *Advances in neural information processing systems* 32 (2019).

we actively choose to ignore organizations and technology that do so. Much like *Brave New World* and *Nineteen Eighty-Four*, we choose entertainment to truth and soma to reality.[10]

The point here is to not merely warn the reader that they could fall victim to fake news but that they are likely already victims of fake news. There are a few things that a wary investor can do defensively:

1. Seek quality information sources and cross-verify as much as possible.

2. Keep a radically open-minded attitude.

3. Try to identify the bias, agenda, and incentive of a particular piece of information.

4. Think critically about every article and piece of news.

5. Be contrarian, i.e., take the opposite viewpoint of whatever narrative is being portrayed or popular opinion.

Early studies in the promulgation of news through social networks showed that certain supernodes (people with a high degree of connections to other people) were highly trusted. We know these supernodes more commonly today as "influencers." I would be wary of information coming from influencers, as they're incentivized by the same mechanisms as mainstream media (i.e., to maximize viewership).

## Being Open Minded

Investing, in general, is a wide and deep discipline that seems as much about a journey of self-exploration as it is about the acquisition of knowledge. In sorting information, we spend much of our time thinking critically about information, but it must also be tempered with open-mindedness. Ray Dalio, in *Principles*,[11] encourages the reader to be "radically open-minded" first and then critical later. Being closed to new ideas (regardless of source) can cause missed opportunities, not only in investment but also in life.

*Example*: If I were a liberal-leaning individual who personally found the personal politics of Peter Thiel abhorrent and therefore excluded reading and

10. Huxley, Aldous. *Brave New World*. DigiCat, 2022; Orwell, George. *Nineteen Eighty-Four*. Secker & Warburg, 1949.

11. Dalio, Ray. *Principles*. Simon and Schuster, 2018.

understanding his investment philosophy, then I'd miss out on the ideas of one of the premier venture capitalists. Similarly, if I were a Republican who fervently believed that George Soros was the devil incarnate, I would miss out on understanding the thinking of an investor at least a generation ahead of his time.

The types of social and mainstream media have a role in shaping our biases. It is well established that different news sources have different consumers and, consequently, different levels of trustworthiness.[12] We already suffer from many unconscious biases. What is the utility of consciously creating new ones?

### High Correlation

Correlation is a statistical measure of how closely two asset prices move together. Mentioned earlier is the idea in portfolio allocations that we should pick non-correlated assets for the purpose of risk mitigation via asset class diversification. Similarly, as we approach basic investing decisions, we should ask ourselves if this has a high or low correlation with the S&P. A large proportion of equities are highly correlated. Correlation can change over time. For instance, BTC (Bitcoin) was considered non-correlated, but in recent years has seen a higher correlation as crypto has become an accepted asset class.

### Average Duration of Economic Recession

As we consider equity investments with high S&P correlation or alternatively buy S&P index funds, it arises as to what is our level of risk? As discussed above, can we quantify an expected value?

We can approach this from two different perspectives: (1) looking at periods of economic decline (i.e. recessions); (2) examining the price action of S&P.

The first case has interesting implications as a participant in the job economy. It's helpful to calculate the amount of emergency funds we might consider keeping in reserve in the event of unemployment. Most personal finance common sense uses three months of living expenses as a rule of thumb. As the below data shows, this may be far short of the buffer that may be desired. Recessions are defined as "a significant decline in economic activity spread across the economy, lasting more than two quarters."

---

12. Sanders, Linley. "Trust in Media 2022: Where Americans Get Their News and Who They Trust for Information." YouGov, 5 Apr. 2022, today.yougov.com/topics/politics/articles-reports/2022/04/05/trust-media-2022-where-americans-get-news-poll..

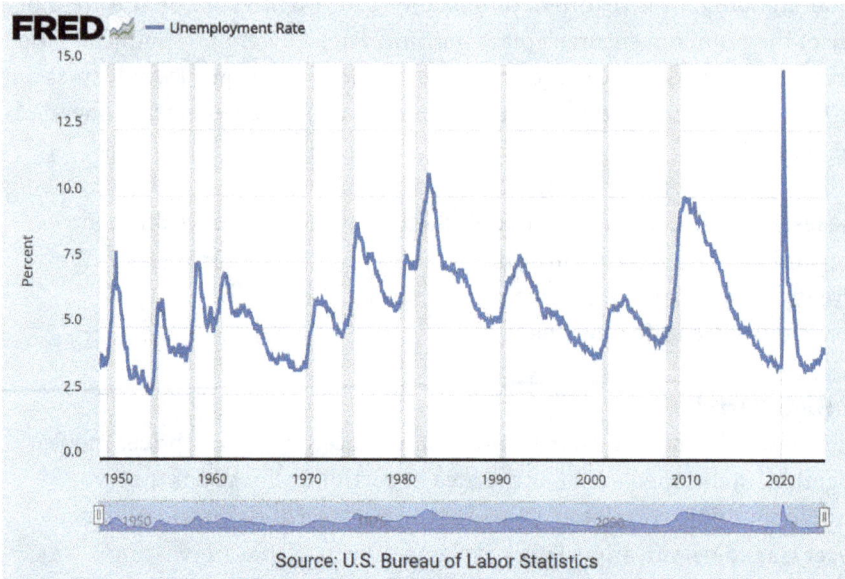

Source: U.S. Bureau of Labor Statistics

Source: U.S. Bureau of Labor Statistics, Unemployment Rate [UNRATE], retrieved from FRED, Federal Reserve Bank of St. Louis; https://fred.stlouisfed.org/series/UNRATE, April 30, 2024.

We might constrain ourselves to the post-WWII era, during which the global balance of power is more similar to present-day than, say, during the American Civil War. A few observations regarding the post-WWII period:[13]

- The longest interval between recessions is 11 years.

- The average interval between recessions is 5.6 years.

- The longest recession was about 1.5 years.

- The average recession duration was 10.8 months.

- The standard deviation recession duration is ~4 months.

---

13. https://en.wikipedia.org/wiki/List_of_recessions_in_the_United_States

If we're in a particularly volatile job market, we might, on average, desire an emergency fund of 11 months. To be extra safe and within two standard deviations, we might want as much as 19 months of emergency savings.

This gives us an idea of the worst-case duration of recession, but we'd also like to know how much we could potentially lose, which brings us to the second perspective – S&P 500 price action during a recession. If we take the S&P 500 prices[14] during a recession on a per-month basis, we get the following table for the peak-to-trough drawdowns.

| Drawdown | % of Time |
|----------|-----------|
| 5%-10% | 13% |
| 10%-20% | 27% |
| 20%-50% | 33% |
| >50% | 13% |

Note that the % of time doesn't sum to 100% that's because the S&P 500 actually increased in price during the post-WWII period of demobilization and high employment. So, it was excluded from this calculation.

Using the above table, we can calculate the expected upper and lower drawdown amounts as a percentage.

- lower end drawdown %: $(.05 * .13) + (.1 * .27) + (.2 * .33) + (.5 * .13) =$ .16 or 16%

- upper end drawdown %: $(.1 * .13) + (.2 * .27) + (.5 * .33) + (.85 * .13) =$ .34 or 34%

---

14. S&P 500 (^GSPC) historical data - yahoo finance. (n.d.). https://finance.yahoo.com/quote/^GSPC/history/ Accessed 3 May 2024.

The results are summarized in the below table.

| Drawdown | % of Time | Low End Drawdown by % | Upper End Drawdown by % |
|---|---|---|---|
| 5%-10% | 13% | 0.65% | 1.30% |
| 10%-20% | 27% | 2.70% | 5.40% |
| 20%-50% | 33% | 6.60% | 16.50% |
| >50% | 13% | 6.50% | 11.05% |
| | | | |
| Expected Value Drawdown | | 16.45% | 34.25% |

The expected value of drawdown during a recession is between 16% and 34%. This calculation is skewed heavily because we're only observing drawdowns during recessions, and the Great Depression of 1929 had a drawdown of 85% from peak to trough, and we include this in the above calculation. This is ok because we're only trying to get a rough estimate of how bad things can get. Like any good engineer, we ought to consider conservative yet realistic tolerances. Landru-forbid, we ever have another Great Depression.

## 3.6 Macroeconomics

The term *macroeconomics* may sound like an intimidating academic subject, but casual readers may take some solace in the fact that there's no Nobel Prize in Economics; rather, there's a Nobel Memorial Prize in Economics. They may take additional comfort that the speculative predictions of professional economists are often no better than those of the casual observer. This is likely why the economy is a popular small-talk topic and the subject of many talking heads in the mainstream media. No one person truly understands the entirety of the national or global economy. A recent NPR radio show likened economics to Asimov's *Foundation* series – a sci-fi trilogy wherein the protagonists develop a theory of predicting human behavior called "psychohistory."[15] Without a grand unified theory of economics, we must acknowledge our limitations in understanding and predictive capabilities of economics in its current state. I suspect as we gain new ways of understanding vast amounts of data via unsupervised machine learning algorithms, many macroeconomic theories will go the way of trephining, or at least evolve to accommodate the vast amounts of data being mined. Despite its many drawbacks, studying the economy yields many helpful conceptual models and correlative metrics. Some of these models and metrics can have limited predictive capabilities or, at the very least, can describe some of the features of the evolving national or global economies.

For instance, measuring M2 (the amount of U.S. dollars in banks) can give at least an idea of how much money is available. As the Fed injected money into the economy during the 2020 Covid pandemic, the M2 supply increased from \$6tn to \$10tn. Inflation was a predictable outcome. This is a good pivot into a natural feature of the national economy: inflation.

## Inflation

Inflation is the idea that the buying power of money tomorrow is worth less than it is today. Even scarier is that the rise of fascism, and eventually WWII, can be linked to hyperinflation in the Weimar Republic.[16] (Note: the reason for the rise of Nazism is a confluence of different factors outside the scope of this book.) Understanding this seemingly boring and ubiquitous feature of our economy is critical.

### "Real" vs. "Nominal" Value

We start with a couple of terms: "real" vs. "nominal." These two terms only make sense in the context of time. Suppose we had a time machine (maybe in the form of a blue police box piloted by an eccentric doctor with two hearts) that allows us to travel between the present and, say, 100 years ago. If we traveled back 100 years, we'd notice that prices for similar goods would be very different, i.e., much lower dollar amounts in the past. For instance, a pair

---

15. Asimov, Isaac. Foundation. Bantam, 1991.

16. Fergusson, Adam. *When money dies: The nightmare of deficit spending, devaluation, and hyperinflation in Weimar Germany.* PublicAffairs, 2010.

of socks in the 1920s would cost about $1.00[17] and would now cost maybe ~$10.00.[18] The dollar value of a product in different time periods is referred to as the "nominal" value.

We calculate the "real" value in terms of a time period's dollar value, or, in other words, we account for inflation in terms of that time period's money. For example, if the cost of a fancy chair today (2023) is $100 and next year (2024) the same chair is $105, and all other things being equivalently increased in price, we could say the inflation increased 5% between 2023 and 2024. The "real" value of the chair next year in terms of this year's dollars is still $100. This is because it's the same chair – what's changed is the value of money, i.e., the $100 has decreased in buying power.

Inflation is measured by the consumer price index (CPI) – a basket of different products. Headline CPI's inflation number is the usually reported inflation number, whereas core CPI is the exclusion of high volatility items such as food and oil. PCE (personal consumption expenditure) is presently becoming a popular alternative to CPI among economists,[19] so it's good to be at least passingly familiar as the favored metric changes over time. Regardless of the chosen metric of inflation, in order to be financially literate and to evaluate economic statements critically, we must take inflation into account and be cognizant of real value in some years' dollar terms. For example, if I recently read an article in a popular financial magazine bemoaning the drop in worker productivity as "plummeting 2.7%" while labor costs increased 6.3%, I could erroneously conclude that worker productivity is dropping while expenses are rising. On the other hand, if I take into account the current CPI of 5.5% at the time of this writing and the fact that just a few months ago CPI was close to 8%, it would be clear that worker productivity is dropping as real wage growth fails to keep up with the rising cost of living.

What are the causes of inflation? The underlying reasons are myriad and oftentimes controversial. Arguments for the underlying cause of inflation may include things such as supply chain bottlenecks, corporate greed, fractional reserve banking (practice of banks required to keep only a fraction of their deposits), and an increase in the money supply.

---

17. https://vintagedancer.com/1920s/advice-for-mens-1920s-clothing-plan

18. https://www.walmart.com/browse/clothing/mens-socks/5438_133197_4033504

19. https://www.stlouisfed.org/publications/regional-economist/july-2013/cpi-vs-pce-inflation--choosing-a-standard-measure

Inflation has some key historical relationships with other macroeconomic indicators, such as the Phillips Curve.[20] The Phillips Curve is the concept of an inverse relationship between unemployment and inflation. As unemployment is low, inflation is high. Intuitively, this can be thought of as more folk are employed, so more money is available to be spent on products (such as premium Earl Grey tea), so prices move higher. A similar related idea is the wage-price spiral[21] where high wages lead to high prices and consequently inflation. Inflation is typically fought by the Federal Reserve by raising interest rates (i.e., the fed funds rate – the rate at which the Fed loans money) or controlling the money supply through quantitative tightening.

### Modern Monetary Theory

Modern monetary theory (MMT)[22] is the idea that a government can print money to fuel its spending and control inflation through other means, such as taxes and spending. This is an important theory to be familiar with because of its implications on monetary policy and its impact on inflation. Proponents of MMT point to how the U.S., as the global reserve currency (we will discuss this definition later), has printed money, and it hasn't produced inflation. MMT is not a mainstream academic theory and does not have a strong evidentiary history to support it. In the aftermath of the Covid monetary response, we see a dramatic increase in M2[23] supply as well as inflation. While it is true that inflation does erode the value of national debt, it does so at the cost of devaluing the dollar. The idea that the USD (US dollar) was somehow special due to its role as a global reserve and, therefore, immune to the inflationary effects of money printing is just plain misguided American exceptionalism. In a globalized economy, inflation isn't a localized national phenomenon; it's a global one.

The U.S. enjoys several significant benefits such as the world reserve currency, but it is erroneous to conflate this with the benefits espoused by MMT. For instance, low inflation from printing USD is the result of high dollar

---

20. Phillips, Alban W. "The relation between unemployment and the rate of change of money wage rates in the United Kingdom, 1861-1957." economica 25.100 (1958): 283-299.

21. https://www.investopedia.com/terms/w/wage-price-spiral.asp

22. https://www.investopedia.com/modern-monetary-theory-mmt-4588060

23. https://www.investopedia.com/terms/m/m2.asp

demand. Gresham's Law[24] is the idea that bad money will chase out the good (i.e., market actors will hoard money with value and transact in money with lower value), so nations will have reserves of USD and other high-value currencies and transact if they can in other denominations. The Fed can print money, and other nations will absorb some of this USD. However, when a large amount of USD is printed (e.g., during a pandemic), this leads to inflation because of the large amount of liquidity (also the fact that other nations were similarly lowering interest rates).

### Bond Yield Curve

The bond yield curve is the bond yields for U.S. treasuries at different maturity durations, e.g., 1, 2, 5, 10, 30 years. The inversion of the bond yield curve, that is, short-term treasuries have a higher rate than long-terms, has historically been a warning indicator of an impending recession. The reason for this is the perception of risk in the short term compared to the longer term causes the cost of borrowing money to be higher in the short term compared to the long term.

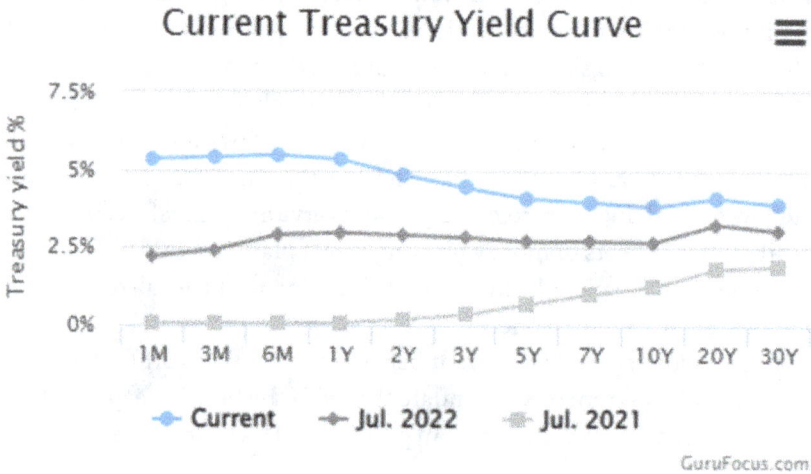

Current Treasury Yield Curve

Source: https://www.gurufocus.com/yield_curve.php

July 2021 reflects a normal yield curve where bonds with longer maturity terms usually have greater risk, so they have higher interest rates. July 2022

24. "Greshams-law." Encyclopædia Britannica, inc. (n.d.).. Encyclopædia Britannica. https://www.britannica.com/money/Greshams-law

reflects a nearly flat but slight inverted yield curve. The current year (2023) reflects an inverted yield curve where short term bonds have higher interest rate than long term, indicating greater short-term risk than long term.

### Historical Treasury Yield Spread (10Y–2Y)

Source: https://www.gurufocus.com/yield_curve.php

## Reflexivity

Macroeconomics is a tricky subject, and George Soros's *Alchemy of Finance* draws from a variety of deep macroeconomic ideas in an informal way. Firstly, he posits that the current price of an asset is a lie, i.e., that the price does not reflect underlying value. Instead, the price embodies the trend and the reflexivity effect. Reflexivity is the idea that there is a feedback loop that is either self-reinforcing (working in the direction of the trend) or self-correcting (working against the trend). Essentially, market participants aren't passive or rational observers of the market but rather take price information into their calculation of perceived value. We see this phenomenon when a "hot" stock gets a lot of attention when its price skyrockets way above a rational valuation. Shiller refers to this as "irrational exuberance," which is the same type of event that led to the Dutch tulip mania that caused the price of tulips to cost as much as a house. Similarly, we see apparent disasters such as Three Mile Island, which caused the owning company (General Public Utilities) to drop to a low of 3.375 in 1979 and rebound to 38 in 1988.[25] Such large dislocations create great market opportunities and highlight the value of contrarian mindsets (thinking contrary to what most people believe).

How does this idea pertain to macroeconomics? Major market participants such as governments, central banks, and other large institutions interact at a high level, both nationally and globally. For example, in the U.S., if inflation is too high, there is political pressure to contain it (because the cost of living of the populace increases). So, the Federal Reserve raises interest rates. The Fed (and the public) see inflation slowing, so it must be working, so they raise interest rates again. Again, inflation slows. Repeat this until unemployment starts to rise, in which case the political pressure works in the opposite direction, and by that time, it's certainly too late to prevent greater-than-expected unemployment. Why does this happen? Firstly, the effects of raising interest rates are delayed, so it's very difficult to time-stopping rate hikes. Secondly, the political incentive is to continue rate hikes or at least appear to be fighting inflation. The political incentives don't reverse until there is an obvious cost. So, large institutions are made of people who have the same mental flaws that make them susceptible to reflexivity. Maybe if we had a soulless AI named Landru from a popular 1966 sci-fi show, we could avoid such events.

Keep in mind that the Fed's interest rates aren't the only macroeconomic levers affected by reflexivity, and we shouldn't be so myopic in analyzing the larger macroeconomic state. There is also trade balance, government spending, government debt, exchange rates, and price of oil. These relationships are complex and change frequently. When Soro wrote *Alchemy of Finance,* he included a model called the Imperial Circle, which outlined these relationships. I think many of the relationships discussed are still relevant today.

### Geopolitics

It is tempting to interpret large geopolitical events and make corresponding investments because geopolitical events are often interventionist – e.g., announcing protectionist policies such as taxes on steel or an outbreak of war between two countries where one of the participants is a significant energy supplier of natural gas. Keep in mind that most news

---

25. Lynch, Peter, and John Rothchild. *One up on Wall Street: how to use what you already know to make money in the market.* Simon and Schuster, 2000.

is public information or that insiders and analysts often have huge time advantages, so the big moves in the market have already been priced in. By the time the average retail investor gets the information, it's usually too late. That's not to say that one can't profit from large price swings in assets such as natural gas during the Russia-Ukraine war, but there's a big difference in investing during the outbreak of war vs. investing in natural gas because of the global energy market state and likelihood of war.

Where retail investors can gain alpha is looking at longer term trends – population growth or political pressures – areas in which the vast majority of mainstream media's attention isn't focused. There are some investors who actually take their sell signals from whether mainstream media is reporting it. For example, consider nuclear energy and an investment in uranium. Nuclear power has a large negative sentiment because of disasters such as Chernobyl and Fukushima. However, relatively few people recognize how much of our current power generation is from nuclear power – i.e., around 18% in the U.S.[26] Additionally, any so-called "green transition" away from carbon fuels will require nuclear power as it currently accounts for 52% of U.S. carbon-free electricity.[27]

We can't entirely neglect large global events because of their large-scale impact. Much like a Disney franchise, involving a mindless galactic civil war, the impact on sci-fi discourse can't be entirely ignored. However, rather than trade on news events we can trade on longer term trends.

### Other Macroeconomic Indicators

Of the many different indicators to choose from, I'll constrain myself to some mentioned in Soros's book.

- U.S. budget deficit: Is the national budget exceeding its revenue, thereby increasing debt?

- Trade deficit: Is the U.S. importing more than it exports?

- Fed funds rate: What rate is the government lending money?

- Exchange rate: Is the dollar increasing/decreasing in strength

---

26. https://www.eia.gov/tools/faqs/faq.php?id=427&t=3

27. https://www.visualcapitalist.com/ranked-nuclear-power-production-by-country/

relative to other currencies?

How are these related? That's a much harder question to answer. Soros gives a pretty good intuitive model in shorthand for how these are related. It suffices for the casual reader to simply know what these indicators are and what direction they're trending. Note that, for the most part, we've constrained our discussion to national macroeconomic indicators. Similar indicators and interactions occur in most modern developed countries, which makes global macroeconomics even more complex.

## 3.7 What is Money?

It's kind of funny that we've gone through this entire book about money without discussing what exactly is money? The response I get most often is, "Money is money; what else is there to know about it?" It helps to have a little bit of history of the USD.

- Prior to the Civil War: States' banks issued their own currencies. Folks and bankers would carry books of different conversion rates, which were unreliable because they'd be out of date almost as soon as they were printed.

- During the Civil War: In order for the federal government to finance the war, it started issuing "Greenbacks" along with war bonds. Because these bonds had a constant rate of return, they had a stabilizing effect on the value of the dollar.

- 1900: The dollar was then backed by the gold standard (i.e., dollars could be exchanged for fixed amounts of gold), which further stabilized its value.

- 1933: Private ownership of gold was prohibited, thereby starting a transition to a fiat currency in the wake of the Depression.

- 1944: Bretton Woods' conference made USD the world reserve currency.

- 1960: Nixon ends the gold standard.

The key takeaway is that the world reserve currency is a fiat currency, meaning that it isn't backed by a physical commodity but rather is backed by full faith in the federal government.

We expect money to have the following qualities:

1. *Store of value:* We expect it to retain its value over time, i.e., its value shouldn't hyperinflate away.

2. *Medium of exchange*: We need some mechanism to exchange currency for something of value, i.e., it should be fungible.

3. *Ledger*: We ought to be able to prove that money changes hands.

The USD certainly fits these requirements. Despite inflation, it retains its value sufficiently that, on a day-to-day basis, we can use it to buy things like streaming services to watch *Lower Decks*[28] and mugs with UFP logos or shirts with fictional wineries. We can prove that dollars changed hands because they move from our bank account to the credit card companies to the bank accounts of the soulless minions of orthodoxy that run Paramount+.[29] The mechanism that enforces the rules of exchange is not only the social contract by which people agree to participate in the economy but also the belief that the government will enforce those rules, i.e., full faith and confidence in the government. In a way, the entire global economy runs on faith in people. Many learned investors expect its imminent demise.

Is cryptocurrency money? Yes, I think it meets the basic requirements of money. Critics might argue that, as a store of value, it fails due to large variance in relation to USD. However, BTC has been around for more than 15 years[30] and has increased in value relative to the USD, which has lost real value. Further, the number of crypto owners has significantly increased. Lastly, the IRS taxes earnings from conversions between different cryptocurrencies.

---

28. https://www.imdb.com/title/tt9184820/

29. https://www.paramountplus.com/

30. Nakamoto, Satoshi (31 October 2008). "Bitcoin: A Peer-to-Peer Electronic Cash System" (PDF). bitcoin.org. Archived from the original (PDF) on 20 March 2014. Retrieved 28 April 2014.

## Active vs. Passive Investing

Active investing means making specific choices regarding assets and timing in one's portfolio. In comparison, passive investing means investing on a regular basis on a fixed set of pre-selected assets. As discussed in a different chapter, most retail investors don't have the resources or time to effectively actively invest, so passive investing in index funds is the recommended approach. This is the accepted common knowledge. What is less understood is that active investing can seem like a money-losing venture for the vast majority of retail investors. In reality, active management can have very high and consistent returns in the hands of skilled professionals. Similarly, passive investing is not as risk-free as most folks believe.

I'm not advocating active management, but it's quite defeatist and simply irrational to believe in something because of majority belief. We also know that some percentage of the population will significantly outperform the market on a consistent basis. It's less well understood that the cause of this success isn't luck or statistics but deterministic behavior and attributes. If it were luck or statistics, we should see a reversion to mean behavior. In the book *Superforecasting*, Philip E. Tetlock studies and identifies several common personality characteristics of superforecasters.[31] They are:

- cautious

- humble

- non-deterministic

- open-minded

- intelligent/knowledgeable

- reflective

- numerate

- pragmatic (that's us!)

- analytical

---

31. Tetlock, Philip E., and Dan Gardner. *Superforecasting: The Art and Science of Prediction*. Random House Business, 2019.

- dragon-eyed – meaning they look at many different perspectives/opinions

- probabilistic

- thoughtful

- intuitive psychologists

- grow/grit mindset (see Carol Dweck).[32]

Additionally, he identifies some other behaviors of superforecasters. They:

- have a tendency for above-average intelligence, though short of genius

- tend toward the "rejection of fate" belief, i.e., on tests whether the outcome was determined by fate

- are detail-oriented and granular

- update their beliefs when presented with new information.

Similarly, Tetlock lays out his ten commandments for improving one's forecasting abilities:

1. triage – focus efforts on high return

2. break a problem into sub-problems

3. get inside and outside views

4. balance under/overreacting to evidence

5. if there are clashing causal forces, look for counterarguments

6. distinguish degrees of doubt

---

32. Claro, Susana, David Paunesku, and Carol S. Dweck. "Growth mindset tempers the effects of poverty on academic achievement." Proceedings of the National Academy of Sciences 113.31 (2016): 8664–8668

7. balance between over/under confidence

8. review errors

9. bring out the best in others and let others bring out the best in us

10. master error balancing.

In his Market Wizards series, J.D. Schwager interviews many successful "market wizards" about their processes and experiences in their investing journey. What stands out to me is that each trader approaches the problem systematically. To be clear, when using the term "system," I'm not merely referring to the system by which the user achieves alpha, but rather the holistic approach with which the investor approaches investment. Not unlike superforecasters, most market wizard systems involve a high degree of self-reflection, a probabilistic approach, and usually some type of risk mitigation. In my opinion, being successful in investing is not about finding the perfect algorithm but finding that algorithm that suits one's psychological preferences and appetite for risk. If one tried to adopt a system that market wizards or superforecasters use, they'd likely fail because they'd likely not understand the internal journey of reaching that point. This is because, as much as we'd like investing not to be based on emotion or human psychology and to have some algorithm to achieve perfect predictions, the reality is that the market has humans and their accompanying irrationality and flaws. However, these flaws and market inefficiencies allow for opportunities that wouldn't otherwise exist in a purely efficient market.

Common knowledge would have us believe that beating the market is a matter of luck. However, at least two popular sources tell us that beating the market is due to a systemic approach and investor attributes. If this is true, why do we believe index investing is the best choice?

Index/passive investing has other problems that are not commonly known. Firstly, because so many passive investors invest in the same products, it causes those assets to be overpriced compared to if they weren't part of a passive investment fund. Secondly, passive investing relies on the idea that the overall trend in the last hundred years is that the stock market will continue to increase in price. A majority of readers will have lived in a period of increasing U.S. prosperity and have a recency bias that blinds them to an economy with continuously shrinking year-on-year real GDP growth, increasingly reliant on Fed liquidity injections.

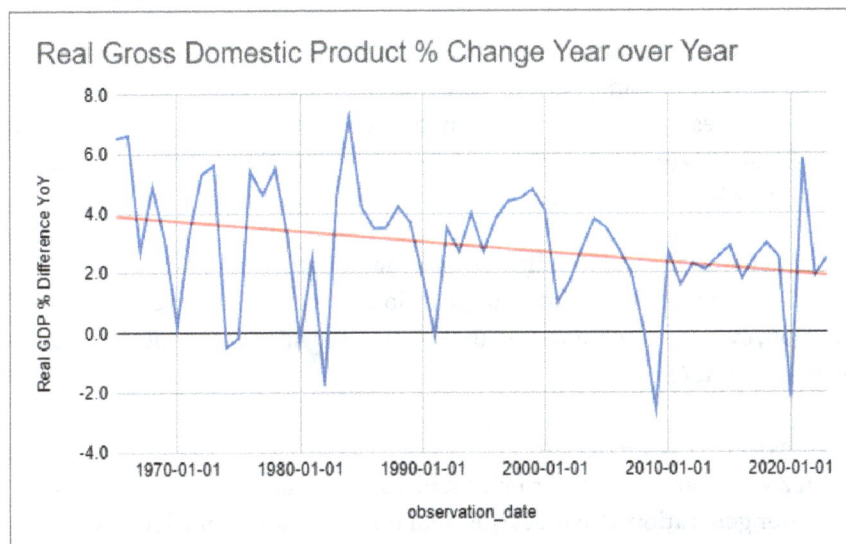

Source: U.S. Bureau of Economic Analysis, Real Gross Domestic Product [A191RL1A225NBEA], retrieved from FRED, Federal Reserve Bank of St. Louis; https://fred.stlouisfed.org/series/A191RL1A225NBEA, May 9, 2024.

**Measuring Success**

In the context of inflation, simply having "more money" may not be a precise enough measurement. A common metric to measure investment success is the Sharpe ratio. The Sharpe ratio is not the only measure, but it's mentioned frequently enough that it's worth defining:

Sharpe Ratio = (Portfolio Return – Risk-Free Rate Return) / (standard deviation of a portfolio)[33]

Let's go through some of the terms.

- Portfolio return: Self-explanatory, i.e., how much is made from an investment.

- Risk-free rate return: If the principle were invested in an alternative risk-free investment, how much would it return? This might be

33. https://www.investopedia.com/terms/s/sharperatio.asp

considered as the U.S. treasury rate or even cash (depending on the economic environment).

- Standard deviation: How much the portfolio fluctuated over the investment time period. Note that the use of standard deviation implies a normal distribution for returns, which is not necessarily a valid assumption since stock prices are usually non-stationary data sets but are probably ok in short time periods.

A higher Sharpe ratio is indicative of a higher return for lower volatility, which is generally good. A low Sharpe ratio may indicate a large standard deviation, even if there's good return the investor might be achieving it at a greater amount of risk.

### Ethics of Investing in ESG

Gen Z voters are more environmentally, socially, and politically conscious than prior generations. To meet this demand, there are a bunch of ESG (environmental, social, government) investment options. On the one hand, there is a clear moral imperative to support companies that strive for good behavior. On the other hand, the amount of money invested by retailers isn't really significant enough to make much of a difference except in aggregate. For example, Chevron isn't going to notice if an individual investor sells their $10k investment (Chevron has a market cap of $290bn). In order to have a 1% impact on the market cap of Chevron alone, there would need to be an order of one million people each changing an investment of $10k.

Additionally, ESG investment options come with a lot of critiques, such as whether they are objectively much better than their counterparts or if the criteria for being "ESG" is appropriately measuring desired good behavior. Or worse, the ESG fund "green-washes" companies, i.e. it acts as a marketing term to make bad actors appear "green."

If one is seeking ESG world-type changes, a better way would be supporting government policy that alters economic incentives. An example would be how investing in carbon credits is not only good for the environment but is also good investing, as these credits accrue in value. In this sense, an ESG investment thesis is more credible in that altered economic incentives encourage the prosperity of ESG-compliant companies.

Whatever the reasoning/intentions behind ethical investing choices on an individual basis, economic incentives usually win out. Encouraging ethical investment choices at the opportunity cost of higher returns is like being a salmon swimming upstream – and the salmon dies in the end! A better and more productive use of investment activism is the support of disruptive startups that engage in ESG-type technologies. Not only do startup investments have potential of large upside returns while promoting the development of market-changing technologies, but they also have strong deflationary effects. This is part of the reason the startup culture in the U.S. is so critical to national long-term economic prosperity.

## Summary

We covered many complex subjects, including:

- Risk and Expected Value

- Efficient Market Hypothesis

- Opportunity Costs

We also covered the basics of doing due diligence via financial statements and the basics valuation via P/E ratio and Market cap.

We also covered some very abstract concepts, such as macroeconomics and the basis of money.

To be clear, each of these subjects could each be several books in their own right. We only explored these concepts as a basis for which a motivated reader could do further investigation, or at least be aware of these subjects as part of their investing conceptual toolbox.

# Chapter 4: Developing Alpha

"Alpha" colloquially refers to better performance relative to another investment. Often, it's in reference to the passive broad index fund investment of an annual 6–8% return. It may also refer to an investment edge over the market, such as knowledge or algorithm. In this chapter, some ideas are outlined for how to develop alpha. This is not financial advice – rather, it's an introduction to additional concepts and information that will allow the reader to start their own lines of inquiry/research/investigation.

## 4.1 Common Alternative Strategies

When I first started researching this area, my first thought was to gather as much price action data as I could and use a machine-learning algorithm to predict their future prices. By taking the most predictable stocks, I could then invest when those prices seemed poised to rise. Of course, this naive approach failed. The price action taken at fine granularity was close to random, and the predictions had a very poor correlation with reality. This was an expensive attempt that took months of coding. It was only years later that I learned the valuable lesson that iterating on ideas is far cheaper than actual iteration in code. For untried ideas that need actual data, then cheap experiments are better than full investment of time in implementation. Now, I look at other people's attempts and examine them critically to see if they're fair experiments and believable outcomes before attempting them myself.

In this section, we review, at a very high level, some popular and conceptually interesting non-traditional investing algorithms/strategies. This is only a high-level review of some of these ideas, and the purpose is to make the reader aware of some of the strategies/algorithms that are popularly deployed.

**Sentiment Trading**

Sentiment is the idea of using some model to classify a statement by sentiment. A sentiment classification could be something as simple as either "positive," "negative," or "neutral."

For example:

| Statement | Sentiment Classification |
| --- | --- |
| This algorithm sucks | negative |
| Data was a great synthetic captain | positive |
| Tell my wife I said "hello" | neutral |

The space of possible sentiment classifications is wide and could even be "bullish" or "bearish." A set of social media tweets classified as bullish could indicate a positive buy signal. Using the latest NLP (natural language processing) techniques with ANNs (artificial neural networks), it is easy to detect sarcasm, toxicity, humor, and even political leaning. The output of an ANN model is usually a probability assigned to the sentiment classification, e.g., 20% negative, 30% neutral, 50% positive, and we'd take the highest percentage as the detected sentiment.

Previously, to train an ANN a large amount of labeled data was needed i.e. a set of statements labeled by the desired classification. Areas with lots of research can leverage open data sets for use in training. Finding well-labeled and clean data for a specific problem continues to be an open problem. Now, with publicly available, more generalized models pre-trained on large data sets, we can use "transfer learning"[1] [2] to fine-tune a smaller dataset specific to our problem domain. To give an idea of scale, I used 1.6 million Twitter statements as training data on a bi-direction LSTM (a type of ANN model) on 1.3 million parameters on a simple sentiment model and got about 82% accuracy.

---

1. https://en.wikipedia.org/wiki/Transfer_learning

2. West, Jeremy, Dan Ventura, and Sean Warnick. "Spring research presentation: A theoretical foundation for inductive transfer." Brigham Young University, College of Physical and Mathematical Sciences 1.08 (2007).

Chris Carmelo, of Dumb Money's YouTube channel fame, used a form of sentiment detection called "social information arbitrage" or "social arbitrage" by examining the usage of different terms in social media and grouping them into tags. Tags that became popular on social media could be used as a signal as to when a product starts gaining popularity and, thus, whether the owning company's stock might be a good purchase.[3]

## Momentum and Mean Reversion Strategies

The momentum and mean reversion strategies are other popular strategies to add to the toolbox. Momentum algorithms attempt to determine if the price is directional, i.e., trending upwards or downwards, whereas mean reversion states that the price action will eventually revert to its mean behavior. Mean reversion is related to trend reversal signals. Both algorithms try to remove the psychological element of trading by relying on quantitative data. A complicating factor in these types of algorithmic approaches is that data is often non-stationary, i.e., the mean changes over time. The Hurst exponent is a common algorithm used in this type of analysis.

## Other Algorithmic Trading Ideas

Algorithmic trading is a really neat idea that ought to have broad appeal to the software community. The problem is that these algorithms are so common now that they're often trading against each other. The analogy I like to use is that of swords and shields, i.e., one firm develops a better sword, and consequently, another firm will develop a better shield – and so on and so on. Software engineers in financial engineering are now quite ubiquitous, and consequently, independently achieving alpha for the typical retail user is very challenging. Going into detail on specific details of each approach, while academically interesting, has low immediate utility. So, I'll summarize some of the relevant ideas and leave further investigation for the interested reader.

- Scree principle component chart
  (https://en.wikipedia.org/wiki/Scree_plot) – helps identify important features of a data set.

- Kalman filters

---

3. Camillo, Chris. *Laughing at Wall Street: How I beat the pros at investing (by reading tabloids, shopping at the mall, and connecting on Facebook) and how you can, too.* St Martin's Press, 2011.

(https://en.wikipedia.org/wiki/Kalman_filter) – assumes a normal distribution to remove noise from a set of data.

- Markov decision processes
https://en.wikipedia.org/wiki/Markov_decision_process) – framework for moving between different states with a certain probability. This can be applied in a lot of different ways to price action.

- Deep reinforcement learning
(https://en.wikipedia.org/wiki/Deep_reinforcement_learning) – uses a neural network to learn different states of a security over a set of different parameters.

## Qualitative Approaches

Although finding alpha algorithmically has become progressively more competitive, we may still find alpha in more qualitative ways. The book *One Up on Wall Street* by Peter Lynch and John Rothchild is full of creative ideas and criteria that can be applied to take advantage of the naive trader's psychological weaknesses. One idea is to invest in what news would consider a major corporate tragedy. Mainstream media has a tendency to hype bad news, and this causes the price action of the corresponding stock to dip lower than a rational valuation of the company and its assets and future prospects. For the same reason, Lynch and Rothchild advise avoiding companies that are viewed most exceptionally favorably by the mainstream or touted as the next Google or IBM.[4]

Like Case Shiller, they reference the P/E ratio as a valuation tool. One interpretation of P/E is the number of years the company would have to operate in order to make its price in earnings, e.g., if NVDA has a P/E ratio of 200, then the expectation is to make its current level of earnings for 200 years. Similarly, FDX has a P/E ratio of 18, so the expectation is for it to make its current earnings for the next 18 years. Which seems more reasonable in terms of pricing? FedEx seems likely to be around for the next 18 years, as implied by the P/E ratio. Whereas NVDA, which competes in a high-tech industry that frequently evolves and reinvents itself, seems less likely to be around for the

---

4. Lynch, Peter, and John Rothchild. *One up on Wall Street: how to use what you already know to make money in the market*. Simon and Schuster, 2000.

next 200 years. As a comparison of longevity, the U.S. has been around for a little less than 250 years. Therefore, FedEx seems to be more fairly priced.

Lynch and Rothchild have some "signs" of what they consider the "perfect stock":

- sounds dull or ridiculous
- does something dull
- does something disagreeable, like cleaning grease traps
- is a spin-off from another business
- institutions don't own it, and analysts don't follow it
- rumors abound, e.g., toxic waste or mafia
- something depressing about it
- no-growth industry
- it's got a niche
- people have to keep buying it, e.g. cigarettes
- user of technology
- insiders are buyers.

They have some similar signs they use as sell signals:

- slow grower: doesn't really buy these
- stalwart: high P/E, new products have had mixed results
- cyclical: costs of a cyclical company start to rise as a result of market conditions, e.g., increased competition
- fast grower: P/E or market cap gets priced significantly higher than seems rational
- turnaround: after its turned around, e.g., Three Mile island second nuclear unit returned to service
- asset: corporate raider (a group that buys a controlling interest at an undervalued price) shows up.

Another good piece of advice they have is to consider how many analysts are watching a particular company. There is probably high knowledge asymmetry, i.e., how likely is it for one to know something the analyst doesn't already know? An individual is far more likely to know something new about a company when there are fewer people studying it. To be clear, this isn't advice to seek insider knowledge. Rather, the point is to be aware of how efficient the market is for that particular company. By that reasoning, taking signals from Jim Cramer, Motley Fool, and other mainstream financial media types is likely a money-losing proposition.

The other reason to introduce some of Lynch and Rothchild's ideas is to demonstrate that a qualitative analytical approach to investing is entirely possible with relatively few rules. As stated in their book, a trader only has to be right about 60% of the time in order to be considered successful.

## 4.2 "To Thy Own Self Be True" or "Know Your Own Psychological Weaknesses"

Most folks are aware of the common adage of not panic-selling when investments take a dip and not getting caught up in the exuberance of a high and refusing to sell, as in the cases outlined in Shiller's *Irrational Exuberance*. This is readily apparent in hindsight and when viewing another's behaviors. But it is far more difficult to recognize this in our own behavior. This isn't a weakness of will or lack of sufficient self-awareness – though it does take a degree of self-awareness to admit we are victims of these tendencies. As noted in *Sapiens*[5] and *Thinking, Fast and Slow,*[6] the evolution of our brains – as we currently understand – is an amalgam of different specialized systems that somehow work together and produce the emergent quality of consciousness - the reader is encouraged to insert any joke about the scarcity of this quality among voting Americans.

Daniel Kahneman defines the interface between these specialized systems and the decision-making process as system 1, thinking fast, and system 2, thinking slow. System 1, thinking fast, is impulsive, based partially on instinct and other biases. System 2, thinking slow, is more deliberate, considered, and hopefully more logical/rational. System 1 is not necessarily worse than System 2 and may actually lead to better outcomes in certain situations – such as a firefighter making a life-or-death decision, a soldier moving on the battlefield, or a day trader buying a dip. System 2 is more deliberate and provides the opportunity to make more logical decisions, but it is often prey to various biases. Ultimately, investors must make decisions about what assets to invest in. Understanding how we make decisions is critical to improving that decision-making process. A critical aspect that's missing

---

5. Harari, Yuval Noah. Sapiens: A brief history of humankind. Random House, 2014.

6. Kahneman, Daniel. Thinking, fast and slow. Macmillan, 2011.

from our general academic curriculum is solid education on how to make decisions. We might think that we've made rational decisions our entire life. The reality is that most of us have very rarely made a completely unbiased choice, nor do we really have a good framework to assess the quality of our decisions. Outlined below are some of the biases that Kahneman describes in his book:

1. Priming: Given an idea first can bias System 1 (fast thinking) towards that idea.

2. Anchoring: Primed towards an arbitrary side, e.g., Gandhi lived to 114 years old, we are anchored to 114 to a higher estimate of his age opposed to an anchor at 35 years old.

3. Availability bias: Bias toward easily recallable or large categories, i.e. planning for disasters is neglected if a disaster isn't in recent memory.

4. Recency bias: more recent events have a higher psychological weighting than events further in the past. This is similar to availability bias in that both types of bias are the result of the brain choosing on the basis of cognitive ease, i.e. it's harder to recall events further in the past or imagine other categories such as disasters that happen infrequently.

5. Statistical insensitive:

   a. insensitivity to prior outcomes

   b. insensitivity to sample size

   c. people do not intuitively think statistically.

6. Confirmation bias: Tendency to see facts to support original conclusion.

7. Blindness to regression to mean: The tendency to ignore the mean or average behavior of some phenomena.

8. Endowment effect: Owning something endows the asset with

greater value such that there is greater pain in giving it up.

9. Overestimation of rare events.

10. Narrow vs. broad framing: Tendency to see a single event vs. one of several events. Narrow framing example: If a coin is flipped and returns heads and basing a decision on that single outcome. Broad framing example: Recognizing that several flips of a fair coin mean that the probability of heads is ½.

11. Experiencing vs. remembering self: Experiencing self only knows the present, whereas the remembering self is what we imagined. Remembering self is unreliable and shouldn't be considered a reliable source of truth.

12. Focusing illusion: Focus is on a particular feature/aspect of some data to the exclusion of other areas.

13. Loss aversion: When making a decision, we have a tendency to avoid loss that is significantly more psychologically painful. We do this at the expense of choices that may have an equivalent or equal expected value.

For these reasons, his conclusion is that even simple formulas for making decisions are better than intuition in making System 2 decisions. Algorithmic trading seems an even better choice for making investment decisions.

## Prospect Theory and the Fourfold Pattern

Prospect theory is the idea that when humans make choices, they value loss and gain differently. Specifically, loss aversion tends to have an outsized effect on decision-making, i.e., folks have a greater emotional response to losses. Tversky and Kahneman[7] found the following tendencies from their studies:

1. Folks will often choose certainty over the possibility of winning. The example fallacy is a court case where there's a 95% chance

---

7. Tversky, Amos, and Daniel Kahneman. "Advances in prospect theory: Cumulative representation of uncertainty." Journal of Risk and uncertainty 5 (1992): 297-323.

of winning, but folk will erroneously choose the certainty of a settlement at a lower-than-expected value.

2. When Faced with a high certainty of loss, folks will take large bets with a small chance of reducing that loss despite the expected value showing the likelihood of a larger loss. This is the behavior where a person is losing gambling in a casino and subsequently makes larger bets in hopes of reducing their losses.

3. Folks have a tendency to make low probability bets with high upside e.g. buying lottery tickets. One might compare this to the long tail investing strategy employed by VC's (Venture Capital). The difference is that the long tail strategy incorporates a high expected value return on investment whereas buying a lottery ticket has a low expected value.

4. Folks will tend to pay a premium for certainty in spite of a high probability of success. An example of this behavior is buying house fire insurance if the probability of fire is relatively low. In fact, insurance companies rely on folks making this miscalculation in order to make a profit. If every potential customer made a completely rational choice, there would be no profit opportunity.

### Removing Bias

Removing bias is tremendously difficult. One way, as alluded to before, is to use an algorithmic approach. What if the algorithm itself unintentionally has bias built in? What if the investing problem isn't amenable to a simple input/output formulation? Suppose the investing problem can generally be composed of an input/output type of problem. Then, the decision to use or trust the algorithm is a human decision. For the moment, let's put aside purely algorithmic approaches and examine decision-making solutions from an analytical perspective.

## 4.3 Rules-Based Decision-Making

Good decision-making processes can apply to investing as well as real life. Adopting a systemic approach to decision-making can also help eliminate the analysis paralysis of particularly indecisive individuals. A good process can eliminate many potential sources of bias and irrationality. Years of psychological study in executive decision-making can be leveraged to improve our personal investing decision-making process. In this section, we try to bootstrap the decision-making system.

From *Thinking, Fast and Slow*, we know there are at least two types of decision-making systems: System 1, which is the fast, intuitive system that helps make life-or-death decisions, e.g., a sword dueler choosing their moves, and System 2, the more deliberate decision-making process. We concern ourselves mostly with System 2, where we assume we have enough time to deliberate on making a sound decision.[8]

The simplest approach, which suffices for most situations, is from Benjamin Franklin – though it probably predates him. This method is simply to list in two columns the pros and cons. Then, systematically remove items from both lists of equivalent weights. Then, go with the column with the most items still remaining.

In his book *Principles*, Ray Dalio of Bridgewater Associates outlines a rules-based approach to making decisions, both in life and investing. Outlined below are some of the key concepts in his book:

- Use believability-weighted information to make decisions.

- Systemize decision-making by operating by a set of principles and always assume missing knowledge.

- Approach to determining principles:

  o seek the smartest people who disagree with you

  o know when not to have an opinion

  o develop/test principles

  o balance risks in ways to keep upside while reducing downside

- Five-step process to succeeding in life goals:

  o have clear goals

---

8. Kahneman, Daniel. Thinking, fast and slow. Macmillan, 2011.

- o identify and don't tolerate the problems that stand in the way of achieving those goals

- o accurately diagnose the problems to get at their root causes

- o design plans that will get around them

- o do what's necessary to push these designs through to results

- Decision-making:

  - o the biggest threat is emotions

  - o learn before deciding

  - o new is overvalued relative to what is currently working well

  - o critical: Identify who to ask questions

  - o balance the cost of knowing more vs. not making decisions

- Decision-making process:

  - o slow down thinking to note decision criteria

  - o write the criteria down as a principle

  - o think about those criteria when we have an outcome to assess and refine them before the next "one of those" comes along

- General life advice:

  - o if a statement starts with "I could be wrong" or "I'm not believable," then that should trigger a follow-up question
  - o use pain as a trigger for quality reflections

A couple of key ideas stand out to me. Firstly, as is consistent with other authors such as Shiller and Kahneman, I hold that emotions are one of the greatest threats to good decision-making and, consequently, investing. If two Nobel laureates consistently say the same thing, then one ought to listen. Secondly is the idea to systematize the decision-making process.

Journaling already has a well-documented history of increasing mindfulness and self-awareness and acts as a helpful reference to improve learning. It is key to making sound decisions to document our current mental state at the point of decision-making.

Let's summarize what we've learned:

1. Humans have so many mental flaws and biases that they are poor decision- makers.

2. A rules-based approach to decision- making helps reduce bias.

3. Recording mental state and decision- making are key to self-reflection and improvement.

## 4.4 Algorithmic Decision-Making

In the book *Algorithms to Live By*,[9] Christian and Griffiths outline several computer science algorithms that can be applied. A few problems/solutions/heuristics they cover:

- optimal stopping

- explore vs. exploit

- sorting

- caching

- scheduling

- networking

- Bayes theorem

- Laplace rule of succession

---

9. Christian, Brian, and Tom Griffiths. *Algorithms to live by: The computer science of human decisions.* Macmillan, 2016.

- game theory

I won't go into too much detail into each of these algorithms as a much better explanation can be easily Googled. However, I will highlight how these algorithms could apply to some investment and life problems.

## Optimal Stopping

Optimal stopping,[10][11] also known as the fussy suitor problem (aka the secretary problem), is framed as the following: Suppose I am only able to date one person at a time and suppose I somehow could one-dimensionally rate a date by some score. Further, having once stopped dating a person and started dating someone new, I can never go back to the same person. How many people should I date before I decide to get married? We don't know the rank of a person or the distribution of ranks in the dating pool. We can only discover this as I begin dating, after which we can make some judgments on the types of people I can date (kidding). As I'm dating, at some point, I must choose what is the threshold over which I'll choose the next highest ranked suitor for marriage (with a 50% divorce rate). Or framed another way: how many people out of my dating pool should I date before I set a threshold?

The answer is unsurprisingly 37%. Just kidding ... sort of ... I'm not going to step through the math but will leave it to the reader to do further reading if interested. There are multiple variants with different solutions, but the classical solution in a low information environment is n/e where n = number of candidates and e = Euler's number.

It should be obvious but, if it's not, here's the disclaimer that this is not dating advice and people ought not make one-dimensional evaluations of each other, nor should an individual attempt to date 37% of all eligible potential partners. On the other hand, stock selection could be amenable to this type of solution. Suppose I have limited time/resources to devote to picking a high return/risk stock with a certain P/E ratio? How many stocks should I research?

---

10. https://en.wikipedia.org/wiki/Optimal_stopping

11. Ferguson, Thomas S. "Who solved the secretary problem?" Statistical science 4.3 (1989): 282-289.

# 4.5 Probabilistic Decision-Making

## 4.5.1 Bayesian Thinking

Bayesian thinking is one of those understated math concepts that is hugely useful when trying to think rationally about the probability of certain events. Understanding its utility and implications is, as Obi-Wan Kenobi put it: "first steps into a larger world" ... a statistical world. We can make observations and calculate the probability of events based on them. This is a deep concept, so I'll only introduce the idea; to gain mastery and deeper utility, it's useful to do further investigation and practice. For those not mathematically inclined, we'll use a hopefully simple example to illustrate its immediate utility.

Bayesian theorem is mathematically stated as follows:

$$P(A \mid B) = P(B \mid A) * P(A) / P(B)$$

Where

A = event
B = data or evidence

$P(A \mid B)$ = probability A given B; a.k.a. "posterior probability"
$P(B \mid A)$ = probability of B being true given A is true; a.k.a. "likelihood"
$P(A)$ = probability of A or the event in question, aka "prior probability"
$P(B)$ = probability of B being true; a.k.a. "normalization constant."

Intuitively, this can be thought of as the probability of the data or evidence being true.

### Example: Where There's Smoke, There's Fire

Suppose we see some smoke in the distance near our house and want to calculate the probability of our house being on fire. We'd reformulate A and B as follows:

A = House on fire
B = Smoke

Bayes's theorem for fire can then be restated as the following:

P (Fire | Smoke) = P(Smoke | Fire) * P(Fire)/P(Smoke)

Let's break this apart:

P (Fire | Smoke) = probability of fire given that there is smoke
P (Smoke | Fire) = probability of smoke given there's a fire

These two statements seem fairly similar but are subtly different.

For "P (Fire | Smoke)": This is the "posterior probability" or value we are trying to determine. Note how a fire is defined as a house on fire. Not all sources of smoke are indicative of a house fire, e.g., smoke could be having a BBQ or smoker or a bonfire or chimney. So this certainly isn't 100% as we might have supposed earlier.

For "P (Smoke | Fire)": This is the "likelihood" or the probability of smoke given there's a fire. Can we estimate this probability? Examining the converse, I can't think of an example of a house fire producing no smoke. So, the probability of smoke being given a house fire must be close to 100%, or effectively so.

P (Fire) = probability of house fire, also known as "prior."

Intuitively, this represents our prior assumption of the probability generally that our house is on fire. We can estimate this if we think about the number of houses we've seen and the number of them having been on fire, I would guess that, unless we've led a particularly tragic life or close with a pyromaniac, this is a pretty low number. Let's say 0.01% or 1/10,000 type of event.

P (Smoke) = probability of smoke, also known as the "normalization constant." We might intuitively think of this probability of data we've gathered.

This is where things get interesting. What is the probability we've seen smoke like that on a given day. Let's suppose we live in suburbia and we observe our neighbors do a BBQ with a smoker a few times every year. So the probability we see smoke is 1/100.

If we plug the numbers into the formula, we get:

P (Fire | Smoke) = (1) (1/10,000) / (1/100) = 0.01 or 1/100

Rephrasing this, there's only a 1/100 chance that, while we were doing this calculation, our house was concurrently burning down. That's pretty good odds that we can take our time.

Now, suppose we lived in an urban environment where it frequently rains, so observing our neighbors' BBQs is much less frequent, e.g., 1/1000.

P (Fire | Smoke) = (1) (1/10,000) / (1/1000) = 0.1 or 1/10

I wouldn't panic, but I'd try to get home a little more quickly. The point is that as our evidence or P (Smoke) changes, we update our belief in the probability of a house fire.

If, for instance, there's a 1/10,000 chance that my neighbor BBQs or doesn't own a BBQ and I see smoke, then that'd indicate an extremely rare event. In this example, P (Fire | Smoke) increases in certainty because P (Fire)/P (Smoke) or (1/10,000)/(1/10,000) = 1. It becomes exceedingly urgent to call the fire department. Intuitively, if we see smoke, and seeing smoke is a low-probability event, then the probability of a house fire is much more likely.

Using conditional probability in this way gives a much more precise estimate or probability of an event than if we chose to use the general probability of our house burning down of 1/10,000 vs. our estimates of 1, 1/10, and 1/100, depending on how likely it is to see smoke in our neighborhood.

The strength in Bayesian thinking is updating our belief P (Fire|Smoke) based on evidence or P (Smoke). Bayesian thinking can be easily applied to investmenting domain. An example might be how P (nuclear meltdown | Ukraine invasion) or P (recession | inverted yield curve) etc.

Note that, up to this point, all of the examples I've given are relatively low-probability events. This perspective needs to be balanced against our intuitive bias against Black Swan events. Black Swan events (coined by

Nassim Talib[12]) are characterized as:

1. lower than average probability of occurring

2. large impact

It's unreasonable to expect Black Swan events to occur all the time, but the probability can be assessed quantitatively and can be planned for appropriately.

### 4.5.2 Laplace's Rule

In *Algorithms to live by,*[13] Christian and Griffiths include Laplace's rule as a simple heuristic to make estimations based on observations. The example they give is that, if we have a pool of tickets with w being winning tickets and n being the number of attempts, we can estimate our chances of pulling the next ticket and winning via: $(w+1)/(n+2)$.

For example, if we observe five winning tickets drawn and ten tries, we can estimate our probability of the next ticket winning as $(5+1)/(10+2) = ½$.

Similar to Bayes's theorem, we can update our probability of winning upon further observations or drawings. So, if we saw six winning tickets in 11 attempts, we'd estimate our probability of winning at $(6+1)/(11+2)=7/13$, i.e., slightly better than 50%.

This rule can be applied to investing in a variety of different ways. For example, suppose there's a mining company with ten possible mining locations, of which only three are viable. The company intends to purchase an additional mining location. What is the probability of that additional location being viable? $(3+1)/(10+2) = 4/12 = ⅓$.

Laplace's rule is just an estimation, and any investment of a serious nature requires due diligence commensurate with the size of the investment and more qualitative analysis. However, it is a simple heuristic to make estimations. In the above example, if the company hypothetically claimed it was going to double its mining output, then an additional mining location may not be sufficient. On the other hand, if they planned to stake another

---

12. Taleb, Nassim Nicholas. The black swan: *The impact of the highly improbable. Vol. 2.* Random House, 2007.

13. Christian, Brian, and Tom Griffiths. *Algorithms to live by: The computer science of human decisions.* Macmillan, 2016.

nine locations, then doubling that revenue becomes more realistic and might be a reasonable bet.

### 4.5.3 Fermi-ize

Fermi-izing is the heuristic of making an estimate of some unknown metric based on adjacent information. It was invented by a physicist named Enrico Fermi, who's famous for his relation to the Fermi paradox.[14] [15] The Fermi paradox is the idea that estimating the heuristic for the likelihood of alien life is relatively high, yet we don't have strong evidence of that life ... yet.

As described in the *Superforecasters* example, suppose we wanted to know how many piano tuners were in the city. We could estimate this by the number of pianos per household and the population of the city. This should give us a pretty good estimate of the number of piano tuners in a given city. For example, if we live in a moderate-sized city of, say, two million, it may take a few hours to tune a piano. Based on the observation that, let's say, we see a piano in every 50 homes or so. Then gives us about 40k pianos (1/50 * 2 million). Let's guess that it takes a few hours to tune a piano (e.g., three hours). So we get about 120k total piano tuning hours needed in a year. If the average American works about 2000 hours a year, then that gives us about 60 piano tuners in the city.[16]

The application to investing seems obvious as the heuristic to estimate, say, the number of instant pots and annual sales revenue of instant brands. As with any heuristic, the usual caveat of required due diligence applies.

### 4.6 DIY Investment Process or "Lambo Money"

This is a little bit of a tongue-in-cheek allusion to all the get-rich guides out there. Following this process will not lead to wealth. It's merely an example of how to remove many of the psychological biases and other investing

---

14. https://en.wikipedia.org/wiki/Fermi_paradox

15. Where is everybody?": An account of Fermi's question" Archived June 29, 2007, at the Wayback Machine, Dr. Eric M. Jones, Los Alamos technical report, March 1985. Jones wrote to Edward Teller on July 13, 1984, Herbert York on Sept. 4, and Emil Konopinski on Sept. 24, 1984.

16. Schoemaker, Paul JH, and Philip E. Tetlock. "Superforecasting: How to upgrade your company's judgment." *Harvard Business Review* 94.5 (2016): 73–78.

fallacies of the casual investor. Any method that proclaims to work for individual A will almost certainly fail due to psychological differences in individual B. Unless individual B has felt the pain of loss of lessons learned by individual A, then it's unlikely that individual B will adhere as strongly to the same rules as individual A. Experience and self-awareness are valuable commodities. So, what is the utility of learning any process here? It's to give the prospective investor a means of bootstrapping their own methodology that they can evolve and iterate that process over time.

Presented in Appendix A is a basic process divided into a couple of sections:

1. main thesis/due diligence

2. psychological checklist.

Section 1 outlines all the typical questions involved in an investment thesis. What are the upsides and downsides? What are the central facts that support an investment opportunity? Can we characterize the management of a company as good or bad? What are the second- and third-order effects of the investment's positive outcomes? What are the risks to the thesis? What's the best medium for capturing value in the thesis?

Section 2 provides a checklist of various biases identified in Kahneman's *Thinking, Fast and Slow*.[17] It also includes questions to calibrate for confidence and mitigate regret. It's important to have a psychological plan after funding an investment if a corresponding price action occurs that may be contrary to expectations or much better than planned. For example, if an investment takes a large dip, we need to be emotionally prepared and not panic sell. Having the plan to accommodate price actions helps mitigate fallacies in System 1, or "fast thinking."

This process isn't meant to be a static process but an iterative tool that adapts to our investment and psychological needs. It cannot be used in simple isolation from reflection and updating of beliefs. It's helpful to record investment choices/perspectives over time to see how the beliefs change, and learning occurs. Lastly, using a checklist by rote won't guarantee success. As with all disciplines, it requires time, patience, and practice in order to

---

17. Kahneman, Daniel. *Thinking, fast and slow.* Macmillan, 2011.

become even moderately consistent. Unfortunately, investing is a rare field where additional work doesn't necessarily translate to a higher degree of success, but we can at least try to mitigate the major sources of errors in the investment decision-making process.

## Summary

In this chapter, we discussed some ideas for developing alpha, such as:

- sentiment analysis

- momentum

- mean reversion

- qualitative analysis

We then discussed many of the psychological fallacies associated with decision-making (such as loss aversion and confirmation bias) and strategies for removing bias.

Lastly, we examined in detail probabilistic decision-making via

- Bayes Theorem

- Laplace's Rule

- Fermi-ization

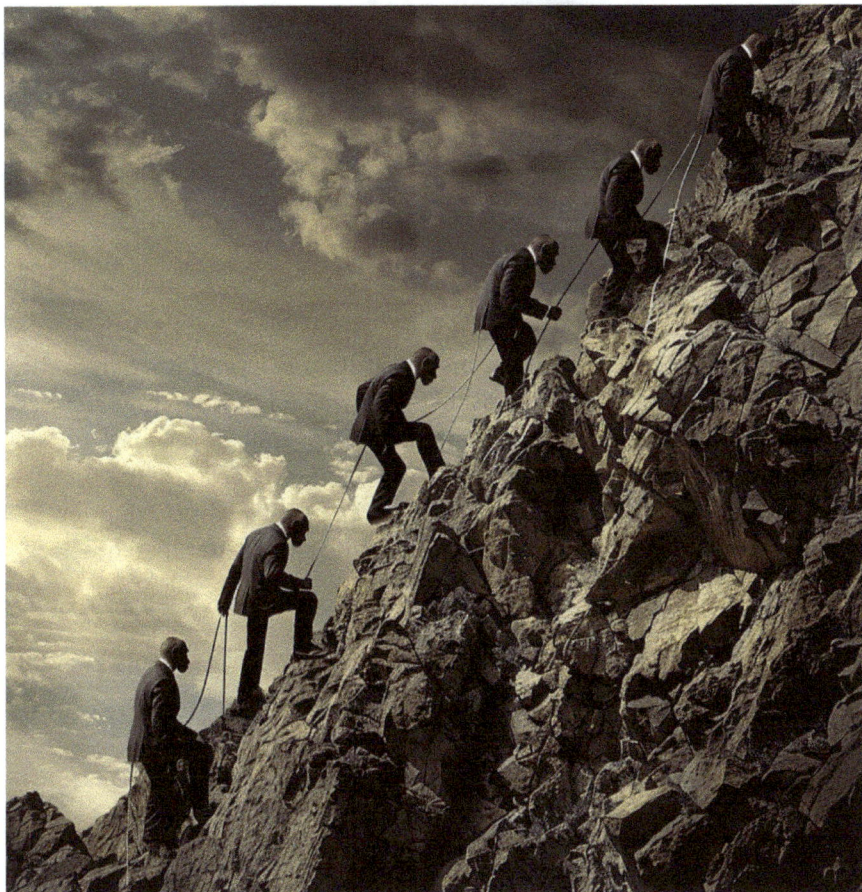

"It's possible to commit no mistakes and still lose. That is not a weakness. That is life." —Jean-Luc Picard, *Stardate 42923.4*[18]

---

18. https://memory-alpha.fandom.com/wiki/Peak_Performance_(episode)

# Chapter 5: Following the Leader

It's not a weakness to admit that some folk are better at certain activities than others. In terms of probability, most of us are probably within three standard deviations of each other in some competency – assuming a standard normal distribution. The reality is that competency in most fields is not normally distributed but is more accurately described as a power law distribution where relatively few individuals perform significantly better than others. These two distributions are illustrated below:

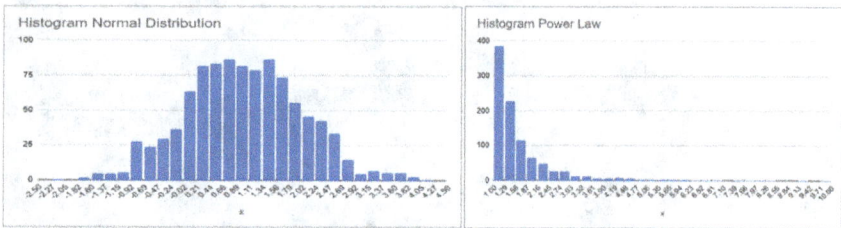

Left: Normal Distribution; Right: Power Law Distribution

This phenomenon is well known in finance as well as nature. For example, the distribution of wealth in countries tends to follow power law distribution. The success of companies in non-zero-sum (winner takes all) markets also tends to follow a power law. For example, consider the market share of search engines. Similarly, for talent, there is a similar distribution where a vanishingly small handful of individuals greatly outperform the rest. These individuals are known in the software industry as the "rock stars" who have 10x the productivity of the rest of us muggles. Similarly, some luminaries far outperform everyone else when investing. It stands to reason that learning from these "rock stars" or aping the habits of these 10x performers can have significant benefits, with the big caveat that a bright young engineer put so eloquently: "If you read a book that Michael Jordan wrote about playing basketball, you still wouldn't be able to play basketball as well as him."

However, if we follow some of the basic things that Michael Jordan does, such as being fit, practicing shooting, being awesome, etc., then we're much better off than our couch-dwelling control group. Similarly, for investing, we ought to practice due diligence, look for alpha opportunities, pay attention to our risk/reward, etc. – we ought to do much better than our smooth-brained ape brethren on Robinhood.[1] By studying these leaders, we can incorporate techniques and perspectives into our own investing framework.

## 5.1 Rock Stars

So, who are these rock star investors? I think everyone's heard of the likes of Warren Buffet, Peter Thiel, and George Soros. Jack Schwager's series on market wizards[2] features interviews with many more of these investors – a cornucopia of information. I can only highlight a very few based on my own predilections/interests. To be clear, this list doesn't diminish the accomplishments or ideas of those not included.

### Benjamin Graham

Graham is primarily famous for having written *The Intelligent Investor*,[3] a classic on value-investing. Graham also wrote *Security Analysis*, another classic, but I'd recommend tackling that if truly dedicated to professional investing as it's said to be even denser than *The Intelligent Investor*. Surprisingly, in the company of influential investors, Graham's net worth is said to be only in the few millions as his primary motivator wasn't the building of wealth. Warren Buffet credits Graham's influence in his investing.

### Warren Buffet

Of the famed oracle of Omaha, is there anywhere to escape the oft-quoted billionaire? At the time of this writing, Buffet is the 7th richest person in the world with a net worth of ~$136bn. His investment style and choices are highly studied. He practices long-term value-based investing. This means he looks carefully at fundamentals such as financial statements, management, and competitive advantage. A lot of the ideas here are discussed in the

---

1. https://www.robinhood.com/us/en/

2. Schwager, Jack D. *Market wizards, updated: Interviews with top traders.* John Wiley & Sons, 2012

3. Graham, Benjamin, and Luke Daniels. *The intelligent investor* rev ed. HarperCollins, 2015.

Due Diligence section earlier in this book. A good resource for further investigation is *Think, Act, and Invest Like Warren Buffett.*[4]

While there is a lot to learn in value investing, one should be cautious of overreliance on a single model of thought. At the time of writing, meme-stocks, meme-coins, and NFT(Non-Fungible Tokens) don't necessarily follow the same rules of value investing. Further, equities commonly have double-digit P/E ratios. The value-investing interpretation is that equities are extremely overvalued and, therefore, would lead to overly conservative investing decisions during times when the S&P continues to increase in value. This highlights an important point: no single model can work in all investing environments. In the post-pandemic, following a value-investing regimen would exclude significant opportunities.

## Peter Thiel

Peter Thiel is known for VC (Venture Capital) investments, has a net worth of $7.3bn and is part of the so-called PayPal mafia. His book *Zero to One*[5] is a really good glimpse into asymmetric investing, i.e., high risk for high return. He looks for opportunities that are the next Google or Facebook. Not surprisingly, involvement in VC necessitates incorporating a "long-tail strategy" where a majority of investments will have middling returns, and maybe 1/100 will have returns that pay for the other investments. So, the premise of *Zero to One* is to look for investments with large asymmetric returns that are 10x or 100x the principle. As a result, investments in this arena are startups. This contrasts sharply with Warren Buffet, who focuses on business fundamentals and value propositions. Venture Capital is an important part of the U.S. innovation engine and shapes the current tech industry. *VC An American History*[6] is a good resource for exploring the historical aspects of VC. Thiel continues to play a large role in startups and VC to this day.

---

4. Swedroe, Larry. Think, act, and invest like Warren Buffett. McGraw-Hill Education, 2012.

5. Thiel, Peter, and Blake Masters. Zero to one: Notes on startups, or how to build the future. Currency, 2014.

6. Nicholas, T. (2020). VC: An American history. Harvard University Press.

### George Soros

Soros, with a current net worth of $6.7bn, famously shorted the Bank of England. His book *Alchemy of Finance*[7] showcases his philosophy of reflexivity, which reinforces and integrates well with the conclusions of *Irrational Exuberance*[8] and *Thinking, Fast and Slow*.[9] As discussed previously in this book, reflexivity is the idea of self-reinforcing feedback loops on trends that work either in a positive or negative direction. *Irrational Exuberance* studies the causes of bubbles which are a form of self-reinforcing feedback loops. One of the major ideas in *Thinking, Fast and Slow* is the types of cognitive fallacies which impact our decision making stills. Many of the macroeconomic ideas in his book were ahead of their time and, I'd argue, are still relevant today. More discussion on how to use macroeconomic relationships is in the Macroeconomics section of this book.

### Stanley Druckenmiller

Druckenmiller worked for Soros at his Quantum Fund and has a net worth of $6.2bn. His average annual return has been 45%. His investment style is similar to Soros's in that he makes a few very large investments. Some of the features of investment style are outlined in his famous Lost Tree Club speech:[10]

- "Put all your eggs in one basket and watch it very carefully."

- "Diversification and all the stuff they're teaching at business school today is probably the most misguided concept everywhere."

- People tend to focus on the present instead of trying to visualize the future; never invest in the present.

- Central banks and liquidity move markets more than earnings.

---

7. Soros, George. The alchemy of finance. John Wiley & Sons, 2015.

8. Shiller, Robert J. Irrational exuberance. Princeton university press, 2015.

9. Kahneman, Daniel. Thinking, fast and slow. Macmillan, 2011.

10. Druckenmiller, S. (2015, January). Stanley Druckenmiller Lost Tree Club. Lost Tree Club. North Palm Beach; Florida.

Druckenmiller credits his performance to the preservation of capital and home runs.[11] Specifically, "home runs" is the idea of betting big when conviction is high. Druckenmiller exhibits an open-mindedness that allows him to take contrary evidence and allows him to rapidly alter the position of his portfolio, as detailed in The New Market Wizards. He exhibits many of the traits in common with Superforecasters.[12]

### David Swensen

Swensen managed Princeton's endowment from $1bn in 1985 to $29bn in 2019. He wrote *Pioneering Portfolio Management*,[13] which is a high-level outline of investment strategy for Princeton's endowment. He followed it up with *Unconventional success*,[14] aimed more at personal investors. Swensen's style and philosophy were outlined early on in Portfolio Construction.

### Ray Dalio

Dalio is the Chief investor of Bridgewater Associates. He's written several books, notably *Principles*.[15] The book *Principles* shares many of the same ideas as *Thinking, fast and slow*. Specifically, *Thinking, Fast and Slow* outlines discuss many of the cognitive fallacies in our decision-making and, therefore, investing framework. Having a rules-based decision-making process removes many of the biases and qualitatively leads to quantitatively better decision-making. In *Principles*, Dalio outlines the specific set of rules or "principles" he uses in decision-making. Interestingly, he uses these principles as a framework not only for management and leadership but also for living life. There are a lot of takeaways and helpful bits of useful advice, such as the high value of interpersonal relationships.

---

11. Schwager, J. D. (2008). The New Market Wizards: Conversations With America's Top Traders. Marketplace Books.

12. Tetlock, Philip E., and Dan Gardner. Superforecasting: The Art and Science of Prediction. Random House Business, 2019.

13. Swensen, David F. Pioneering portfolio management: An unconventional approach to institutional investment, fully revised and updated. Simon and Schuster, 2009.

14. Swensen, David F. Unconventional success: A fundamental approach to personal investment. Simon and Schuster, 2005.

15. Dalio, Ray. Principles. Simon and Schuster, 2018.

Principles probably isn't the best book to learn about investing, but in the absence of a personal rational decision-making framework, it can be a useful template. A rational, evolvable, and generalized decision-making system that is also simultaneously aligned with our personal principles is a high bar. However, developing such a system has high utility investing as well as personal decision-making. Those who have a good framework will be at a significant advantage in making investing and life decisions. The good news is that such a system is a teachable skill. Having the discipline to abide by system outcomes is an entirely different problem.

### Chris Camillo

Camillo is one of the early adopters of the social arbitrage strategy. He was heavily influenced by *One Up on Wall Street*.[16] At the time of this writing, he has a YouTube channel called "DumbMoney"[17] and he's also featured in Jack Schwager's *Unknown Market Wizards*. Social Arbitrage is the investing strategy of examining social media trends in order to gain a predictive information edge in company performance. For example, if a significant number of influencers are excited about a specific energy drink or shoe brand, then that company may have large earnings that might later translate into a higher stock price. Most institutional investors don't study influencer behavior for a good reason. Imagine an analyst citing a TikTok video or YouTube comment section as part of their thesis for investing millions in the next bobblehead doll of a famously bald starship captain.

Camillo has trading traits similar to other highly successful investors such as Druckenmiller and Soros, where he makes large, concentrated investments. The best way to learn about social arbitrage is through his book *Laughing at Wall Street*.[18]

An important takeaway from Camillo is his approach to risk. One of the major advantages of professional investors over retail investors is the amount of risk they can take. As high returns correlate with high risk, successful investors tend to be more profitable than comparably correct retail investors.

---

16. Lynch, Peter, and John Rothchild. One up on Wall Street: how to use what you already know to make money in the market. Simon and Schuster, 2000.

17. https://www.youtube.com/@DumbMoneyLive

18. Camillo, Chris. Laughing at Wall Street: How I beat the pros at investing (by reading tabloids, shopping at the mall, and connecting on Facebook) and how you can, too. St Martin's Press, 2011

To obviate this advantage, Camillo uses his "Big Money Account" to separate high-risk assets from safer assets (such as retirement funds). This separation of assets allows him to make short-term concentrated trades. Both books mentioned in this section provide excellent insight and ideas for achieving an investing edge over Wall Street.

### John C. Bogle

Bogle, the founder of the Vanguard Group, is a large advocate of passive investing funds. Vanguard Group has on the order of $7 trillion under management as of this writing. Vanguard funds have among the lowest fees in the industry. So called "Bogle-heads" are those that adhere to the strictures of passive investing.

The general argument for passive investing is two-fold. Firstly, casual investors do not have adequate time to professionally manage their investments. And secondly, a majority of professionally managed funds underperform the market. Therefore, it stands to reason that passive investing is appropriate for casual retail investors. If you're reading this book, you probably find the second reason suspect. Similar to the efficient market hypothesis, it supposes that a given investor falls into the category of underperforming the market. Accepting this assumption without evidence is simply irrational.

### Additional Thoughts on Following Rockstars

Following some of these investors via 13F filing (a form that institutional investors have to fill if they manage $100m or more) or websites that follow their trades is helpful in developing alpha. Further, understanding their investment philosophy, far from a purely academic pursuit, is rich in pragmatic application. Speculative ideas are put to the test in the most rigorous manner: real life. The reason that investing is so interesting is the similarity to all deep intellectual pursuits that lead to the inevitable realization of the connectedness of mathematics, philosophy, human nature, and that numinous quality of reality: chance!

## 5.2 Additional Resources

Resources and documents frequently go out of date, but here's my go at it:

- Investopedia:[19] really good wiki for basic terminology and concepts

- Coursera:[20] Don't be afraid to learn something new!

- NerdWallet:[21] Great reference for personal finance number

- Polymarket:[22] Prediction market

- Planet Money:[23] Great podcast on economic events

- The Indicator:[24] U.S. macroeconomic news

- *Thinking, fast and slow:*[25] In my top three books of my lifetime to read

I have a bunch more references in my bibliography. I recommend a quick walkthrough as some of them I would consider classics in investing.

## 5.3 Feedback and Call to Action

If you enjoyed this read, found it helpful, or learned something new, then do a public good and recommend it to friends or family. Or send comments, corrections, feedback and questions to justin.masui@gmail.com because it will make this book better and helps all of us on our financial journey. Thanks for reading!

---

19. https://www.investopedia.com/

20. https://www.coursera.org/

21. https://www.nerdwallet.com/

22. https://polymarket.com/

23. https://www.npr.org/sections/money/

24. https://www.npr.org/podcasts/510325/the-indicator-from-planet-money

25. Kahneman, Daniel. Thinking, fast and slow. Macmillan, 2011.

# Appendix: Investing Worksheet

## Section I: Main Thesis/Due Diligence

**Qualitative Questions:**

- Background/Description:

- Upside expected value (note: 1. can try fermi-ize to get estimates 2. use single-digit precision) A: _____

- Downside risk A: _____

- Other investors: A: _____

- What are some third-order effects of thesis (most people stop at 2) A: _____

- Are there any relevant predictions in polymarket.com A: _____

- Founders:

- Customer demand? A: _____

- Competition? A: _____

- Inflation/Deflation? A: _____

- Supplier concentration? A: _____

- Industry publications? A: _____

- Financial analysis? A: _____

- Management positioning?

- Recent management changes? A: _____

- Credentials of management seem solid? A: _____

- General long-term prospects (3–5 years)? A: _____

- Financial strength & capital structure acceptable? A: _____

- Dividend record? Note: high dividends have opportunity costs in reinvestment

- Current dividend rate? A: _____

- Competitive advantage? A: _____

- What is the best way to capture value? A: _____

- Is it better to wait? A: _____

- What price seems fair for the market cap? A: _____

- Have I identified unknowns and turned them into actionables? A: _____

## Basic Price Analysis:

- What is its market cap? A: _____

- How much correlation to S&P? A: _____

- Historical valuations? A: _____

- Comparable valuations (i.e., market cap with other similar companies)? A: _____

- What is the P/E? A: _____

- Short interest? A: _____

- Shareholder concentration? A: _____

- M&A rumors? A: _____

**Good Signs:**
- Has wide moat/competitive advantage

- Marathoner vs. sprinter, i.e., steady growth

- Sows and reaps, i.e., spends money on developing business

**Warning Signs:**
- Not serial acquirer

- Not opm addict (other people's money)

- Not johnny-one-note, e.g., relying on a single customer

**Risk Checklist:**
- Investment contains assets? i.e., tangible or other otherwise?

- Can I afford this drawdown for 3+ months?

- Would I be willing to hold for 10 years of recession?

- Does it have a valid safety margin?

- Does leadership have a good history of making money/success?

- No significant macro risks?


# Section II: Psychological Checklist

- Not timing the market/speculating

**Questions to Ask for Calibrated Confidence:**
- How much experience do I have? What is my track record with similar decisions in the past?

  - A: _____

- What is the typical track record of other people who have tried this in the past?

- o A: _____

- If I am buying, someone else is selling. How likely is it that I know something that this other person (or company) does not know?

  - o A: _____

- If I am selling, someone else is buying. How likely is it that I know something that this other person (or company) does not know?

  - o A: _____

- Have I calculated how much this investment needs to go up for me to break even after my taxes and costs of trading?

  - o A: _____

## Questions to Ask for Anticipated Regret

- If I'm right, I could make a lot of money. But what if I'm wrong? Based on the historical performance of similar investments, how much could I lose?

  - o A: _____

- Do I have other investments that will tide me over if this decision turns out to be wrong? Do I already hold stocks, bonds, or funds with a proven record of going up when the kind of investment I'm considering goes down? Am I putting too much of my capital at risk with this new investment? When I tell myself, "You have a high tolerance for risk," how do I know? Have I ever lost a lot of money on an investment? How did it feel? Did I buy more, or did I bail out?

  - o A: _____

- Am I relying on my willpower alone to prevent me from panicking at the wrong time? Or have I controlled my own behavior in advance by diversifying, signing an investment contract, and dollar-cost averaging?

○ A: _____

## Mitigating Bias

- Am I affected by herding bias?

- Am I avoiding a painful realization?

- Am I making any major assumptions/ideas?

- Do I have a reciprocation tendency? I am not letting benefits from the company affect me.

- Am I affected by loss aversion?

- Have I sought outside advice with high believability when poor alignment?

- Cognitive ease – is this System 1 vs System 2?

- Am I suffering from glucose deficiency?

- Am I affected by priming (having an idea prior to a decision which is biased towards that idea)?

- Am I affected by anchoring (primed towards an arbitrary side, e.g., Gandhi lived to 114 years old. Now you're biased or "anchored" to 114 – a higher estimate of his age)?

- Am I affected by availability heuristic (bias toward easily recallable or large categories? i.e. planning for disasters is neglected if not one in recent memory)?

- Have I accounted for my tendency toward statistical insensitivity?

- Am I affected by confirmation bias (tendency to see facts to support original conclusion)?

- Am I affected by blindness to regression to the mean?

- Am I affected by endowment-effect (owning something endows it with greater value such that greater pain giving it up)?

- Am I falling into the fallacies of the four-fold pattern of taking risks?

- Am I overestimating rare events?

- Am I broad framing outcome vs narrow framing?

- Have I accounted for the experiencing vs remembering self?

- Have I accounted for focusing illusion (tendency to focus on certain ideas to the exclusion of others)?

## Section III: Editorial on Crypto Currency

Cryptocurrency is fraught with disinformation. The incentives for this are myriad and go directly, in some cases, to geopolitics and the ability of nation-states to project soft power through economics. How is this the case? Consider for the moment that the total world supply of USD as measured by M2 is around $20tn and that the crypto market cap is around $1.5tn. Consider further that crypto is a parallel financial system that can easily and quickly move millions of dollars in a fraction of the time of the traditional banking system. Cryptosystems can completely bypass banks, thereby disrupting the traditional banking system. Crypto is faster at moving money than the traditional finance system. Additionally, there are nascent crypto projects that enable other traditional financial products, such as loans and interest-bearing mechanisms (e.g., staking). These products directly disrupt traditional banks' revenue and regulatory role and are a strong threat. It's no wonder the incentive to discredit crypto is so strong.

Let's discuss the two major disinformation campaigns. Firstly, crypto is bad for the environment, and secondly, crypto is used for money laundering. While it is true that the first generation of crypto relies heavily on electricity and uses a lot of hardware, subsequent generations are far more efficient. Recently, on the Ethereum network, the biggest transition is from "proof of work" to "proof of stake," where network participants show that they have a stake in the network vs. proving that they did the hashing work for verification. This innovation significantly reduces electrical power consumption and hardware requirements. Solana is already on proof of stake, as is Avalanche.

The second big disinformation piece is that crypto is used for money laundering and crime. This is true … but then so is USD, and at a far larger scale – drug dealers aren't busted with a bunch of crypto keys, but with cash! USD is used for far more crime and is a lot less easy to track compared to crypto, where most transactions on a crypto network are public (the exceptions are some networks such as Monero, which provide greater anonymous transactions). Additionally, moving money out of a crypto network requires going to an exchange such as Coinbase to convert it to USD. These exchanges act as endpoints and are required to use KYC (know your customer), meaning that withdrawals from networks aren't anonymous – i.e., their utility as a laundering mechanism is severely compromised.

# Bibliography

## Books

Asimov, Isaac. *Foundation*. Bantam, 1991.

Bengen, William P. "Determining Withdrawal Rates Using Historical Data." *Journal of Financial Planning* 7.4 (1994): 171–180.

Camillo, Chris. *Laughing at Wall Street: How I Beat the Pros at Investing (by Reading Tabloids, Shopping at the Mall, and Connecting on Facebook) and How You Can, Too*. St Martin's Press, 2011.

Christian, Brian, and Tom Griffiths. *Algorithms to Live By: The Computer Science of Human Decisions*. Macmillan, 2016.

Claro, Susana, David Paunesku, and Carol S. Dweck. "Growth Mindset Tempers the Effects of Poverty on Academic Achievement." *Proceedings of the National Academy of Sciences* 113.31 (2016): 8664–8668.

Cooley, Philip L., Carl M. Hubbard, and Daniel T. Walz. "Retirement Savings: Choosing a Withdrawal Rate That is Sustainable." *AAII Journal* 20.2 (1998): 16–21.

Cooley, Philip L., Carl M. Hubbard, and Daniel T. Walz. "Sustainable Withdrawal Rates from Your Retirement Portfolio." *Financial Counseling and Planning* 10.1 (1999): 39–47.

Covey, Stephen R. *The 7 Habits of Highly Effective People*. Simon & Schuster,

2020.

Dalio, Ray. *Principles*. Simon and Schuster, 2018.

Fergusson, Adam. *When Money Dies: The Nightmare of Deficit Spending, Devaluation, and Hyperinflation in Weimar Germany*. PublicAffairs, 2010.

Finke, Michael S., Wade D. Pfau, and David Blanchett. "The 4 Percent Rule is Not Safe in a Low-Yield World." Available at SSRN 2201323 (2013).

Graham, Benjamin, and Luke Daniels. *The Intelligent Investor* rev ed. HarperCollins, 2015.

Harari, Yuval Noah. *Sapiens: A Brief History of Humankind*. Random House, 2014.

Hershfield, Hal E., and Daniel M. Bartels. *"The Future Self."* The Psychology of Thinking About the Future. The Guilford Press, 2018: 89–109.

Himmelstein, David U., et al. "Medical Bankruptcy in the United States, 2007: Results of a National Study." *American Journal of Medicine* 122.8 (2009): 741–746.

Huxley, Aldous. *Brave New World*. DigiCat, 2022

Kahneman, Daniel. *Thinking, Fast and Slow*. Macmillan, 2011.

Kelley, Amy S et al. "Out-of-Pocket Spending in the Last Five Years of Life." *Journal of General Internal Medicine* 28.2 (2013): 304–309. doi:10.1007/s11606-012-2199-x

Lynch, Peter, and John Rothchild. *One Up on Wall Street: How to Use What You Already Know to Make Money in the Market*. Simon and Schuster, 2000.

Nicholas, T. (2020). *VC: An American History*. Harvard University Press.

Orwell, George. *Nineteen Eighty-Four*. Secker & Warburg, 1949.

Taleb, Nassim Nicholas. *The Black Swan: The Impact of the Highly Improbable.* Vol. 2. Random House, 2007.

Schwager, Jack D. *Market Wizards, Updated: Interviews with Top Traders.* John Wiley & Sons, 2012.

Schwager, J. D. (2008). *The New Market Wizards: Conversations with America's Top Traders.* Marketplace Books.

Schwager, Jack D. *Unknown Market Wizards: The Best Traders You've Never Heard Of.* Harriman House Limited, 2020.

Shen, Kristy, and Bryce Leung. *Quit Like a Millionaire: No Gimmicks, Luck, or Trust Fund Required.* Penguin, 2019.

Shiller, Robert J. *Irrational Exuberance.* Princeton University Press, 2015.

Soros, George. *The Alchemy of Finance.* John Wiley & Sons, 2015.

Swedroe, Larry. *Think, Act, and Invest Like Warren Buffett.* McGraw-Hill Education, 2012.

Swensen, David F. *Unconventional Success: A Fundamental Approach to Personal Investment.* Simon and Schuster, 2005.

Swensen, David F. *Pioneering Portfolio Management: An Unconventional Approach to Institutional Investment, Fully Revised and Updated.* Simon and Schuster, 2009.

Tetlock, Philip E., and Dan Gardner. *Superforecasting: The Art and Science of Prediction.* Random House Business, 2019.

Thiel, Peter, and Blake Masters. *Zero to One: Notes on Startups, or How to Build the Future.* Currency, 2014.

Zellers, Rowan, et al. "Defending Against Neural Fake News." *Advances in Neural Information Processing Systems* 32 (2019).

## Papers

Elliott, Elaine S., and Carol S. Dweck. "Goals: An Approach to Motivation and Achievement." Journal of Personality and Social Psychology 54.1 (1988): 5.

Kruger, Justin, and David Dunning. "Unskilled and Unaware of It: How Difficulties in Recognizing One's Own Incompetence Lead to Inflated Self-assessments." Journal of Personality and Social Psychology 77.6 (1999): 1121.

Mathews, George B. "On the Partition of Numbers." Proceedings of the London Mathematical Society 1.1 (1896): 486-490.

Norton, Michael I., and Dan Ariely. "Building a Better America—One Wealth Quintile at a Time." Perspectives on Psychological Science 6.1 (2011): 9-12.

Phillips, Alban W. "The Relation Between Unemployment and the Rate of Change of Money Wage Rates in the United Kingdom, 1861-1957." Economica 25.100 (1958): 283-299.

"Where is Everybody?": An Account of Fermi's Question" Archived June 29, 2007, at the Wayback Machine, Dr. Eric M. Jones, Los Alamos technical report, March 1985. Jones wrote to Edward Teller on July 13, 1984, Herbert York on Sept. 4, and Emil Konopinski on Sept. 24, 1984.

Tversky, Amos, and Daniel Kahneman. "Advances in Prospect Theory: Cumulative Representation of Uncertainty." Journal of Risk and Uncertainty 5 (1992): 297-323.


## Websites

"529 Plan Basics." WA529 Washington College Savings Plans, wastate529.wa.gov/basics. Accessed 30 Oct. 2023.

Alpha, Contributors to Memory. "Emergency Medical Holographic Program."

Memory Alpha, Fandom, Inc.,
memory-alpha.fandom.com/wiki/Emergency_Medical_Holographic_progra
m. Accessed 30 Oct. 2023.

Alpha, Contributors to Memory. "Peak Performance
(Episode)." Memory Alpha, Fandom, Inc., memory-alpha.
fandom.com/wiki/Peak_Performance_(episode). Accessed 30 Oct. 2023.

Alpha, C. to M. (n.d.). Vulcan salute. Memory Alpha.
https://memory-alpha.fandom.com/wiki/Vulcan_salute

Banton, Caroline. "Wage-Price Spiral: Definition and What
It Prohibits and Protects." Investopedia, Investopedia,
www.investopedia.com/terms/w/wage-price-spiral.asp. Accessed 30 Oct.
2023.

Bhutada, Govind. "Ranked: Nuclear Power Production, by
Country." Visual Capitalist, 19 Jan. 2022, www.visual
capitalist.com/ranked-nuclear-power-production-by-country/.

Board of Governors of the Federal Reserve System (US), Share of Total
Net Worth Held by the Bottom 50% (1st to 50th Wealth Percentiles)
[WFRBSB50215], retrieved from FRED, Federal Reserve Bank of St. Louis;
https://fred. stlouisfed.org/series/WFRBSB50215, April 20, 2024.

Bhutada, Govind. "The Rising Cost of College in the U.S." Visual Capitalist, 4
Feb. 2021, www.visualcapitalist.com/rising-cost-of-college-in-u-s/.

Bullard, James. "CPI vs. PCE Inflation: Choosing a Standard Measure: St.
Louis Fed." Saint Louis Fed Eagle, Federal Reserve Bank of St. Louis, 9 Dec.
2021,
www.stlouisfed.org/publications/regional-economist/july-2013/cpi-vs-pce-
inflation-choosing-a-standard-measure.

Chait, Jonathan. "A Peek into the Fantasy World of the
Persecuted Rich." Intelligencer, 25 Sept. 2012, nymag.com/
intelligencer/2012/09/fantasy-world-of-the-persecuted-rich.html.

"Current US Yield Curve Today (Yield Curve Charts)." GuruFocus, www.gurufocus.com/yield_curve.php. Accessed 30 Oct. 2023.

"Deep Reinforcement Learning." Wikipedia, Wikimedia Foundation, 10 Sept. 2023, en.wikipedia.org/wiki/Deep_ reinforcement_learning.

"Degrees, Certificates, & Free Online Courses." Coursera, www.coursera.org/. Accessed 30 Oct. 2023.

"Doctor Who." Wikipedia, Wikimedia Foundation, 27 Oct. 2023, en.wikipedia.org/wiki/Doctor_Who.

Do the rich pay their fair share? Federal Budget in Pictures. (2024, March 21). https://www.federal budgetinpictures. com/do-the-rich-pay-their-fair-share/

"Dumb Money Live." YouTube, YouTube, www.youtube.com/@DumbMoneyLive. Accessed 30 Oct. 2023.

D'Souza, Deborah. "Modern Monetary Theory (MMT): Definition, History, and Principles." Investopedia, Investopedia, www.investopedia.com/modern-monetary-theory-mmt-4588060. Accessed 30 Oct. 2023.

"Gresham's law." Encyclopædia Britannica, Inc.(n.d.). Encyclopædia Britannica. https://www.britannica. com/money/Greshams-law

*Federal income tax rates and brackets.* Internal Revenue Service. (n.d.). https://www.irs.gov/filing/federal-income-tax-rates-and-brackets. Accessed: April 26, 2024

"Fermi Paradox." Wikipedia, Wikimedia Foundation, 30 Oct. 2023, en.wikipedia.org/wiki/Fermi_paradox.

Fernando, Jason. "Sharpe Ratio: Definition, Formula, and Examples." Investopedia, Investopedia, www.investopedia. com/terms/s/sharperatio.asp. Accessed 30 Oct. 2023.

Fientist, The Mad. "Traditional IRA vs. Roth IRA – the Best Choice for Early Retirement." Mad Fientist, 23 Feb. 2022, www.madfientist.com/traditional-ira-vs-roth-ira/.

"Frequently Asked Questions (Faqs) – U.S. Energy Information Administration (EIA)." Frequently Asked Questions (FAQs) – U.S. Energy Information Administration (EIA), www.eia.gov/tools/faqs/faq.php?id=427&t=3. Accessed 30 Oct. 2023.

Gonzalez, Sarah, et al. "What Has Been Driving Inflation? Economists' Thinking May Have Changed." NPR, NPR, 12 May 2023, www.npr.org/2023/05/11/1175487806/corporate-profit-price-spiral-wage-debate.

"Historical Federal Individual Income Tax Rates & Brackets, 1862-2021." Tax Foundation, 31 July 2023, taxfoundation.org/historical-income-tax-rates-brackets/.

"The Indicator from Planet Money." NPR, NPR, www.npr.org/podcasts/510325/the-indicator-from-planet-money. Accessed 30 Oct. 2023.

Investopedia, Investopedia, www.investopedia.com/. Accessed 30 Oct. 2023.

"Kalman Filter." Wikipedia, Wikimedia Foundation, 24 Sept. 2023, en.wikipedia.org/wiki/Kalman_filter.

"Knapsack Problem." Wikipedia, Wikimedia Foundation, 25 Oct. 2023, en.wikipedia.org/wiki/Knapsack_problem.

"List of Recessions in the United States." Wikipedia, Wikimedia Foundation, 28 Sept. 2023, en.wikipedia.org/wiki/List_of_recessions_in_the_United_States.

"Make All the Right Money Moves." NerdWallet, www.nerdwallet.com/. Accessed 30 Oct. 2023.

"Markov Decision Process." Wikipedia, Wikimedia Foundation, 24 May 2023, en.wikipedia.org/wiki/ Markov_decision_process.

"Mens Socks in Mens Clothing: Brown." Walmart.Com, www.walmart.com/browse/clothing/mens-socks/brown/5438 _133197_4033504/Y29sb3I6QnJvd24ie. Accessed 30 Oct. 2023.

Mint. "Managing Money, Made Simple." Mint, mint.intuit.com/. Accessed 30 Oct. 2023.

Nakamoto, Satoshi (31 October 2008). "Bitcoin: A Peer-to-Peer Electronic Cash System" (PDF). bitcoin.org. Archived from the original (PDF) on 20 March 2014. Retrieved 28 April 2014.

"Nuclear." Energy.Gov, www.energy.gov/nuclear#:~:text=Nuclear%20power%2C%20the%20use%2 0ofthe%20electri city%20generated%20in%20America. Accessed 30 Oct. 2023.

"Optimal Stopping." Wikipedia, Wikimedia Foundation, 3 Sept. 2023, en.wikipedia.org/wiki/Optimal_stopping.

"Paramount Plus: Stream Movies, Shows & Live TV." Paramount+, www.paramountplus.com/. Accessed 30 Oct. 2023.

"Planet Money." NPR, NPR, www.npr.org/sections/money/. Accessed 30 Oct. 2023.

"Refund/Cancellation Policy." WA529 Washington College Savings Plans, wastate529.wa.gov/GET-Refund-Policy. Accessed 30 Oct. 2023.

"Retirement Topics – Required Minimum Distributions (Rmds)." Internal Revenue Service, www.irs.gov/retirement-plans/plan-participant-employee/retirement-topi cs-required-minimum-distributions-rmds. Accessed 30 Oct. 2023.

"Rocket Money – Take Control of Your Money." Rocket Money – Take Control of Your Money, www.rocketmoney.com/. Accessed 30 Oct. 2023.

S&P 500 (^GSPC) historical data - Yahoo Finance. (n.d.).
https://finance.yahoo.com/quote/^GSPC/history/ Accessed 3 May 2024.

Sanders, Linley. "Trust in Media 2022: Where Americans Get Their News and
Who They Trust for Information." YouGov, 5 Apr. 2022,
today.yougov.com/topics/politics/articles-reports/2022/04/05/trust-media-
2022-where-americans-get-news-poll.

"Scree Plot." Wikipedia, Wikimedia Foundation, 2 July 2023,
en.wikipedia.org/wiki/Scree_plot.

Sessions, Debbie L., "What Did 1920s Men's Clothing Cost?" Vintage Dancer,
vintagedancer.com/1920s/advice-for-mens-1920s-clothing-plan/. Accessed
30 Oct. 2023.

"Star Trek: Lower Decks." IMDb, IMDb.com, 6 Aug. 2020,
www.imdb.com/title/tt9184820/.

Summary of the latest federal income tax data, 2024 update. Tax Foundation.
(2024, April 2). https://taxfoundation
.org/data/all/federal/latest-federal-income-tax-
data024/#:~:text=High%2DIncome%20Taxpayers%20Paid%20the%20
Majority%20of%20Federal%2 20taxes.

Team, The Investopedia. "M2 Definition and Meaning in the Money Supply."
Investopedia, Investopedia, www.investopedia.com/terms/m/m2.asp.
Accessed 30 Oct. 2023.

Thier, Jane. "American Worker Productivity Is Declining at the Fastest Rate
in 75 Years-and It Could See CEOS Go to War against WFH." Fortune, Fortune,
5 May 2023,
fortune.com/2023/05/05/remote-work-productivity-5-straight-quarters-
decline-gregory-daco/.

U.S. Bureau of Economic Analysis, Real Gross Domestic Product
[A191RL1A225NBEA], retrieved from FRED, Federal Reserve Bank of St. Louis;
https://fred.stlouisfed.org/series/A191RL1A225NBEA, May 9, 2024.

U.S. Bureau of Labor Statistics. (2024, April 25). *Bureau of Labor Statistics Data*. U.S. Bureau of Labor Statistics. https://data.bls.gov/timeseries/CUUR0000SEEB01?output_view=data.

U.S. Bureau of Labor Statistics, Unemployment Rate [UNRATE], retrieved from FRED, Federal Reserve Bank of St. Louis; https://fred.stlouisfed.org/series/UNRATE, April 30, 2024.

"Wealth Inequality in America." YouTube, YouTube, 20 Nov. 2012, www.youtube.com/watch?v=QPKKQnijnsM.

Wong, Wailin, et al. "How Asimov's 'Foundation' Has Inspired Economists." NPR, NPR, 17 July 2023. www.npr.org/2023/07/17/1188203986/how-asimovs-foundation-has-inspired-economists.

"The World's Largest Prediction Market." Polymarket, polymarket.com/. Accessed 30 Oct. 2023.

"Ynab." YNAB, www.ynab.com/. Accessed 30 Oct. 2023.

## Speeches/Presentations

Druckenmiller, S. (2015, January). Stanley Druckenmiller Lost Tree Club. Lost Tree Club. North Palm Beach, Florida.

West, Jeremy, Dan Ventura, and Sean Warnick. "Spring research presentation: A theoretical foundation for inductive transfer." Brigham Young University, College of Physical and Mathematical Sciences 1.08 (2007).

# About the Author

Justin grew up in Honolulu and subsequently left that sunny island paradise for the dark rainy wind-swept vicissitudes of the Pacific Northwest in Seattle, where he attended University of Washington. He majored in both Industrial Engineering and Applied Computational Mathematical Sciences and minored in Math. He then walked the path of Industrial Engineering, System Administration and entrepreneurship, before getting his master's in computer science from Seattle University, where he published his thesis in the proceedings of the 42nd International Conference on Parallel Processing for his paper "Backing Up Your Data to Cloud: Want to Pay Less." He worked in a variety of corporate technical lead roles before ascending to a Principal Engineer role. He continues to study ML/AI and enjoys performance/optimization problems.

He married his beautiful wife on the beaches of Waimanalo. He loves to travel and has literally circumnavigated the world. He enjoys backpacking, running, swimming, and gaming. Mostly, he enjoys overconsuming unhealthy amounts of science fiction and shortbread cookies.

He bought his first stocks more than 20 years ago (turning 100% profit on energy) and has been actively investing ever since.

www.ingramcontent.com/pod-product-compliance
Lightning Source LLC
Chambersburg PA
CBHW050631190326
41458CB00008B/2228